RECLAIMING MANHOOD

RECLAIMING MANHOOD

A 12-Step Journey to Becoming the Man God Meant You to Be

Dr. David Hawkins & Ross A. Tunnell III

VICTOR BOOKS

A DIVISION OF SCRIPTURE PRESS PUBLICATIONS INC.
USA CANADA ENGLAND

Editor: Greg Clouse
Cover Designer: Scott Rattray
Interior Illustrations: Al Herring

Library of Congress Cataloging-in-Publication Data

Hawkins, David, Dr.
  Reclaiming manhood / David Hawkins, Ross A. Tunnell III.
    p.   cm.
  ISBN 1-56476-027-8
  1. Men—Religious life. 2. Men (Christian theology)
3. Twelve-step programs—Religious aspects—Christianity. I.
Tunnell, Ross A. II. Title.
  BV4843.H368 1992
248.8'42—dc20

                                                 92-18144
                                                  CIP

---

1 2 3 4 5 6 7 8 9 10 Printing/Year 96 95 94 93 92

Table of Contents

Preface

Once I (Ross) purchased a swing set with the words "Some Assembly Required" printed on the box. Eager to get it set up, I dumped the parts on the lawn and proceeded to build. The project went very well. I had only one small difficulty with the large crossbeams—I couldn't get the holes to match up. After forcing them as far as I could, I had to resort to getting my drill and *making* them fit. It wasn't until I set the swing set up on its legs that I saw what I had done. I had unknowingly reversed the two top crossbeams, so that the legs that were angled outward were on the inside and the straight vertical poles were on the outside, right next to the sawhorse swing. Thus, when the kids swung on the sawhorse, they had to hold their elbows in tight, or else they would hit the support pole. Since I had forced the top, I couldn't undo it. The kids continued to bang their elbows, until we finally trashed the whole thing.

It was obvious that I should have followed the instructions. In my hurry to get the swing set up, I tossed the enclosed instructions aside. My male pride said, "I can handle this." By disregarding the Parts List and Instruction Booklet, I was saying in effect, "I know better than Sears how to put this swing set together."

Unfortunately, many of us men have carried the same arrogance into our businesses, marriages, and families. For instance, we didn't follow God's instructions for getting married, and we thought we knew better than God how to put our marriages together. Then we are surprised to discover that things aren't going too well and we wonder why we keep "banging our elbows." When the pain gets too great, we scrap the whole thing and try to build another one.

Reclaiming Manhood is a Parts List and Instruction Booklet for men. Until the last year or two little has been written about needs unique to men. Women's issues have been openly discussed for years, while men's issues have not. It is into this void that this workbook seeks to make a contribution.

It is our conviction that God created us, and He knows best how we ought to function. Marriage and family is God's idea, and He has given us *the* Instruction Book— the Holy Bible. When we violate scriptural principles, there are consequences. When we don't function according to God's design, we are dysfunctional. It is the design of this workbook to help men recover biblical functionality. As a guide for applying the Scriptures, we are using *The Twelve Steps of Alcoholics Anonymous.*

The process of "working the Twelve Steps" has been around for some time now, helping thousands to recover from lives of addiction and dysfunctionality. Because of the severity of those problems, jobs, marriages, and lives have been destroyed. The Scriptures, combined with the Twelve Steps, provide a powerful recovery tool and offer a way to undo the damage done and return us to useful, productive lives.

Reclaiming Manhood is designed to encourage greater understanding of the major issues facing us men in our lives, as well as to apply solutions to problem situations. Some of these men's issues are:

- Work
- Fitness
- Family of Origin
- Marriage
- Power
- Intimacy
- Ethics
- Image/Impression Management
- Money
- Faith
- Sex
- Friendships
- Empathy
- Family

This workbook can be used alone for individual study and application. But the real benefit of the workbook will be realized in a men's support group. There is accelerated growth when we are able to verbalize our feelings and interact with other men. The support and encouragement of a group of men enable us to take steps of obedience that are nearly impossible when tried alone.

Ultimately, this workbook is a by-product of our own men's support group that meets every Friday at noon to work through the Twelve Steps. We are excited about the potential of this workbook. We know how our lives have been benefited as we are on the road to recovery.

The illustrations used in this workbook come from our own experiences and the experiences of the men in our group. When privacy demands it, the identifiable factors in each illustration have been changed so that anonymity is protected. Any similarity to any situation you know personally is coincidental and unintentional. However, because our dysfunctionality is so pervasive, we all have identified with each other and have seen ourselves in each other's experience. We would expect that would be true of our readers as well.

At this point we would like to especially thank our wives, Diane Hawkins and Parmelee Tunnell, for putting up with our dysfunctionality and for giving us the room we needed to grow and to face these issues in our own lives and in our marriages.

The Twelve Steps of Alcoholics Anonymous

1. We admitted we were powerless over alcohol—that our lives had become unmanageable.

2. Came to believe that a Power greater than ourselves could restore us to sanity.

3. Made a decision to turn our will and our lives over to the care of God as we understood Him.

4. Made a searching and fearless moral inventory of ourselves.

5. Admitted to God, and to another human being the exact nature of our wrongs.

6. Were entirely ready to have God remove all these defects of character.

7. Humbly asked Him to remove our shortcomings.

8. Made a list of all persons we had harmed, and became willing to make amends to them all.

9. Made direct amends to such people wherever possible, except when to do so would injure them or others.

10. Continued to take personal inventory and when we were wrong promptly admitted it.

11. Sought through prayer and meditation to improve our conscious contact with God as we understood Him, praying only for knowledge of His will for us and the power to carry that out.

12. Having had a spiritual awakening as the result of these steps, we tried to carry this message to alcoholics, and to practice these principles in all our affairs.

Reprinted with permission of Alcoholics Anonymous, World Services, Inc.

The Twelve Steps of Alcoholics Anonymous and Scripture

1. We admitted that we were powerless over our sin—that our lives had become unmanageable.

   "I know nothing good lives in me, that is, in my sinful nature. For I have the desire to do what is good, but I cannot carry it out" (Romans 7:18).

2. We came to believe that a power greater than ourselves could restore us to sanity.

   "For it is God who works in you to will and to act according to His good purpose" (Philippians 2:13).

3. We made a decision to turn our wills and our lives over to the care of God as we understood Him.

   "Therefore, I urge you, brothers, in view of God's mercy, to offer your bodies as living sacrifices, holy and pleasing to God—which is your spiritual worship" (Romans 12:1).

4. We made a searching and fearless moral inventory of ourselves.

   "Let us examine our ways and test them, and let us return to the Lord" (Lamentations 3:40).

5. We admitted to God, to ourselves, and to another human being the exact nature of our wrongs.

   "Therefore confess your sins to each other and pray for each other so that you may be healed" (James 5:16a).

6. We were entirely ready to have God remove all these defects of character.

   "Humble yourselves before the Lord, and He will lift you up" (James 4:10).

7. We humbly asked Him to remove our shortcomings.

   "If we confess our sins, He is faithful and just and will forgive us our sins and purify us from all unrighteousness" (1 John 1:9).

8. We made a list of all persons we had harmed and became willing to make amends to them all.
"Do to others as you would have them do to you" (Luke 6:31).

9. We made direct amends to such people wherever possible, except when to do so would injure them or others.
"Therefore, if you are offering your gift at the altar and there remember that your brother has something against you, leave your gift there in front of the altar. First go and be reconciled to your brother; then come and offer your gift" (Matthew 5:23-24).

10. We continued to take personal inventory and, when we were wrong, promptly admitted it.
"So, if you think you are standing firm, be careful that you don't fall!" (1 Corinthians 10:12)

11. We sought through prayer and meditation to improve our conscious contact with God as we understood Him, praying only for knowledge of His will for us and the power to carry it out.
"Let the word of Christ dwell in you richly" (Colossians 3:16a).

12. Having had a spiritual awakening as the result of these steps, we tried to carry this message to others, and to practice these principles in all our affairs.
"Brothers, if someone is caught in a sin, you who are spiritual should restore him gently. But watch yourself, or you also may be tempted" (Galatians 6:1).

Reprinted with pemission of Recovery Publications, San Diego, California.

One

Men, Coming of Age

"Why isn't it working?" Jim asked soberly. We had been in the same couples' Bible study for four years with the same six couples. This year two of the couples divorced and another is currently separated. But what really upset Jim was that our Bible study leader is to be brought before the church next Sunday for church discipline. Apparently he has been having an affair while leading our group through a workbook on Christian marriage and family life!

In your life, have you ever wondered why it isn't working? The fact that you picked up this workbook is a pretty good indicator that you have asked that or a similar question. Thousands of men throughout the world are beginning to awaken to the fact that life is not working out like they thought it was supposed to. Many are wanting to know what changes they can make to turn things around. Working through a book like this one is one way men can initiate change.

Unfortunately, it often takes a crisis to wake us up. Today, if you want to make changes in your life, chances are good that you have "hit bottom" in some way. But what matters now is that you want to change. If it is any consolation, you are not alone. Many men are recognizing that their lives are not working. Their lives are not functioning properly—they are dysfunctional; that is, they have "impaired or abnormal functioning."

Now is an exciting time for men. We are finally giving ourselves permission to talk openly about some of our struggles, our fears, even our feelings. Previously, to be a man has meant to be tough, silent, ready to fight—what some call the "John Wayne syndrome." We have family backgrounds of isolation which set us up to have few meaningful relationships as adults. We have backgrounds of chemical dependency and codependency, which also set us up to pass along those traits to the next generation. John Friel, a Minnesota psychologist, says, "You see the castrated male who's nice on the outside but full of rage underneath. You see a lack of fathering" (*Focus*, October/November 1990, p. 40).

Another leader in the current "men's movement," James Hillman, says, "The American male is very often passive aggressive—passive on top and aggressive underneath" (*Focus,* October/November 1990, p. 21). Men are often "under active" to their internal feelings. When asked what we are feeling, we will either say that we don't know, or we will be very quick to give a thought. It is not easy for us to identify our feelings. We are not called upon to do it very often. It is foreign to us to think about our feelings, our needs, our desires. We are too busy doing the things men are supposed to be doing: fathering children, earning a paycheck, fixing our homes, harvesting food.

This workbook is about insight, understanding, education, and self-awareness. It is through this process that we can alter the rigid patterns which have been set in place and start learning to talk about who we are and where we have been. Most men will not engage in this process, and so will never understand who they are, where they have been, and where they are going.

Shepherd Bliss, a professor of men's studies at JFK University, however, says, "Our society expects much from men as providers, protectors, warriors, and initiative takers. Each family and individual then adds its load to a man—perhaps making him into a work object, a security blanket, or Mr. Fix It, able to solve all problems. The taboo against a man's self-reflection on masculinity and subsequent re-evaluation, remains strong in this culture" (*Changes,* October 1990, p. 38).

It is well understood and accepted that we become who we are as a product of our genetic heritage and our family and cultural background. Men in different cultures behave in different ways. We learn *how to behave* and *how to be* "on the job." That is, it is as we watch our fathers and our friends' fathers that we figure out our roles. But because we have *learned* how to be a man, we can change that learning. We can acquire new information. We can update our memory banks, so to speak. And in doing so, we can gain relief.

Now let's explore how our particular culture has influenced us. Your honesty with yourself and willingness to look long and hard within will yield great rewards.

Self-Exploration

● What does it mean to you to be a MAN? _____

_____

_____

_____

● What are manly characteristics? _____

_____

_____

● What is your favorite TV sitcom or drama? _____

_____

● How are the men in that program portrayed? _____

_____

_____

● Who are the male role models in your life? _____

_____

_____

● Describe your relationship with your father: _____

_____

_____

_____

_____

Men in the Scriptures

When we look into the Scriptures, we see a different image of men. Actually, we have many different examples from which to choose. Perhaps the most well-rounded example of a man comes to us from David. Here we see a man who was strong and brave. Certainly we see the "Warrior" in David. He was out to conquer, as so many of us are too. He knew what he wanted and let nothing get in his way. His behavior was motivated by greed and lust. Yet we also can see his vulnerability. He definitely made some wrong choices—his involvement with Bathsheba and the killing of her husband, Uriah (see 2 Samuel 11). But the Scriptures tell us that David was sorrowful for his behavior and had a heart for God. He is an example of a man of God who was "fully human." Can you relate to David with his desire to get ahead, his lust, and yet his sensitivity and remorse?

Peter is another interesting character. Here we find a man who had a fervent faith. He really wanted to follow the Lord. However, he didn't seem to appreciate or recognize his humanity. He denied his weaknesses, and they caused him to stumble, creating even more trouble for him in the long run. The Scriptures show Peter as being impulsive, driven by whim rather than self-discipline. He rushed into situations when caution would have been more appropriate. When he wanted something, he went after it with a passion. Can you identify with him?

Of course, our best example of masculinity comes from what we can glean from the example of Christ. He is our perfect model, whom we can strive to be like; yet we recognize that we can only make progress toward that goal. He seemed to have the qualities of strength, decisiveness, and compassion (Matthew 9:36). He never put others down in order to reach His goals. He was not concerned about image. Rather, He wanted to be true to who He was and to fulfill His mission. He also despaired at times and grew weary, needing rest. He knew that He could only do so much, and developed a game plan to accommodate this fact. The Gospels let us walk with Him in His final months, as He reached out to many, hoping to give them "living water" (John 4:10).

• With which biblical character do you most readily identify? _____

Why? _____

_____

_____

• When David was about to die, he gave a final charge to his son Solomon. His final words include his instructions on what it was to be a man. Read 1 Kings 2:1-4 and write out what David says about being a man: _____

_____

_____

_____

Step One Application

We admitted we are powerless over our sin—that our lives have become unmanageable.

"I know that nothing good lives in me, that is, in my sinful nature. For I have the desire to do what is good, but I cannot carrry it out" (Romans 7:18).

"Why am I so God-awful angry?" Jeff yelled. "I'm out of control. She pushes all my buttons. How can she have so much power over me? She makes me; she breaks me. I crave her approval and affection, but her criticism and coolness devastate me. What's wrong with me? I feel like a puppet on a string."

Jeff's face reflected anguish as he recounted the story. Again, their usual argument had gotten out of hand. Jeff had stormed out of the house. It was always the same. He wanted more affection than Julie was wanting to give. She felt Jeff's sexual needs were more than any red-blooded American girl could supply. The phrase that always set him off was, "Sex is not a basic need. Jesus was the perfect man and He lived without it."

This refusal was the final straw. This time something gave way inside of Jeff. He knew something had to change. Discouraged, depressed, and with thoughts of suicide, Jeff decided to go for help. It wasn't hard to convince Jeff of the truth of the First Step; his life was clearly out of control.

However, it is not always that easy. Sometimes it is very hard to admit that our lives have become unmanageable. This runs contrary to everything that our culture teaches us about being strong. It also runs contrary to many self-help books that tell us that we can achieve anything that we can imagine. It is very tempting—even addicting—to believe that we can do it all. What a thought! But for growth to happen, we must be willing to admit that we need help. *We cannot do it alone!*

Most of us have backgrounds of compulsive behavior. This means that we have not been able to voluntarily change the course of our lives. We do not need to feel ashamed about this. That's the nature of the beast. Lets look at compulsive behavior:

Compulsive behavior is the product of two forces in our lives; our natural desires: (1) to increase personal pleasure, and (2) to eliminate personal pain.

At the risk of oversimplification, allow us to illustrate. Let's suppose that Joe is hurting over a relationship in which he doesn't feel admired or appreciated. As he comes to the weekly sales meeting at work, the receptionist comments, "My, don't you look good. Is that a new suit?" "Well, ah, yes, thank you," Joe stammers self-consciously as he enters the boardroom. Well, as Joe sits down, how does he feel? How would you feel? Joe feels good; he enjoys compliments. Don't you? Since he was already hurting, the compliment meant more to him than it ordinarily would. OK so far.

Now let's jump a week ahead. Joe is getting dressed for the weekly sales meeting, and he can't find his new suit. He feels anxious and asks his wife, "Where is my new suit?" "Oh, I took it to the cleaners," she answers. Now Joe is really upset. Why? Because, to a limited extent, he has already become compulsive about wearing that suit to the weekly sales meeting. Why?

Here is another way to ask the same questions. If Joe knows he is going to pass by the receptionist who complimented him on his suit, and he is particularly needy again that day, which suit will he most likely wear? The new one. Why? Because Joe wants to get another compliment to help dull his personal pain. That dynamic, in a simplistic way, is the cause of all compulsive behavior.

Here are some common "cause and effect" characteristics of compulsive behavior:

1. Compulsive behavior gives a rush of good feelings that is mood-altering, thereby making it addicting;
2. The purpose of the mood-altering agent such as sex, work, chemicals, food, is to ease our personal pain;
3. The relief we experience is only temporary, therefore we use the mood altering agent more and more;
4. Our preoccupation with and our greater use of the mood-altering agent causes problems in other areas of our lives;
5. Our fear of losing our pain killer causes us to deny there is a problem;
6. Eventually, there is a breakdown, which is called "hitting bottom."

All too often it takes "hitting bottom" before we can admit to ourselves that we are powerless over the effects of sin. Some examples of "hitting bottom" include:

1. In the marriage: divorce, separation, or an affair
2. On the job: stressed, fired, or demoted
3. Health: sickness or nervous breakdown
4. Excessive indebtedness or bankruptcy
5. Getting arrested for immorality or illegality

It requires great courage and the help of God to face our denial and to withdraw from our compulsive behaviors. It requires support. It requires asking for help, which is so hard for many of us. It goes against our desire to be self-sufficient. Healing begins as we reach out to others, acknowledging that we can no longer manage our lives, and that we need them and God in new ways.

● In light of this discussion, what are some of the ways you have used pleasure to cover up personal pain?_____

_____

_____

_____

_____

● Have you "hit bottom" in any of the ways listed?_____
If yes, briefly describe your situation. If no, briefly describe why your life has become unmanageable: _____

_____

_____

● What are some habits that you can't seem to break?_____

_____

_____

● What are two of your biggest regrets? _____

_____

_____

Powerlessness does not mean passivity. It means turning our wills over to God to enable us to be the creation He wants us to be.

"But those who hope in the Lord will renew their strength. They will soar on wings like eagles; they will run and not grow weary, they will walk and not be faint" (Isaiah 40:31).

Professional Experience

In my (Dave's) counseling practice and in my own experience, I have found that men cannot talk about their feelings. They are simply unable to talk in those terms. It is not from lack of desire to do so, but from the lack of modeling and experience. We, as men, are taught to talk about sports, machinery, and politics. We are taught, indirectly, not to talk about our feelings.

I am aware, as a professional psychologist, that it takes work for me to talk about my feelings, though it is something I encourage in others every day. I am discouraged at the lack of opportunities for me to honestly share how my life is going. I have had to actively seek out special places, i.e. men's groups, where I will be able to share personal experiences. If I do not aggressively seek out those opportunities, I find myself slowly pulling back inside myself. Furthermore, it is in the sharing of my true self, that I maintain my own well-being.

It is interesting to watch most men, as they gather in groups, try to relate honestly to each other. Not surprisingly, it takes some time to trust one another and get past surface chit-chat. It appears far easier to talk about "safe" topics than about ourselves. Women seem to be able to do this more readily than men. Thank God, the time has arrived when men, in small bits and spurts, are willing to experiment with sharing themselves with one another. I hope we will have patience as we carve out a path for ourselves.

Recovery Affirmations

Most of us are used to beating ourselves up with mistakes from our past. We have made many, so we have a lot of ammunition with which to hurt ourselves. We are familiar with hurling insults at ourselves, and so stopping it takes concentration and a new set of thoughts to repeat to ourselves. It has been found to be tremendously helpful to find words of affirming truth to repeat daily to ourselves, and this is an important part of recovery.

A wonderful beginning step is to consider and meditate on the fact that we have been created in the image of God. Consider that man, each of us, was created uniquely. We see in Psalm 139 and Genesis 1 several important things for us to reflect on. Read daily, for one week, Psalm 139:13-16 and Genesis 1:26-28 and affirm that:

- I have been uniquely and wonderfully made;

- God made me in His image, to mirror and represent Him;

- God made me to need others;

- Through the help of the Holy Spirit, I am empowered to relate effectively to God, to my neighbors, and to nature.

Prayer for Serenity

God, grant me the serenity
to accept the things I cannot change,
the courage to change the things I can,
and the wisdom to know the difference.
Living one day at a time,
enjoying one moment at a time;
accepting hardship as a pathway to peace;
taking, as Jesus did,
this sinful world as it is,
not as I would have it;
trusting that You will make all things right
if I surrender to your will;
so that I may be reasonably happy in this life
and supremely happy with You forever in the next.
Amen.

Reinhold Niebuhr

Two

Men — Power, Approval, Success, and Image

Power! Success! Think about it. Isn't that what the media presents as the ideal situation for a man? The media bombards us with the picture of a tall, dark, handsome man who is able to manipulate situations and people at his command. The stereotype shows this man getting to the top and, while at the top, getting anything he wants. Of course, part of getting to the top means climbing on others to get there. "It's a dog eat dog world, you know." "May the best man win." "Winning isn't everything; it's the only thing." These are a few of the competitive comments made by those scratching and clawing to get to the top. What most don't realize is that this struggle for power and approval is addicting and empty. It takes more and more to gain the illusion of satisfaction. The more power we get, the more we want, and the less it satisfies. We resort to unethical means to gain power and approval. That is when we begin to doubt our worthiness, and we fear that if the truth were known, we would lose the success and approval we are seeking.

At age 35, Bill is a millionaire. He owns several retail businesses and an advertising firm. He buys his clothes and cars based on the image they produce. He is admired in the community as a financial wizard, and his advice and counsel are sought by other businessmen. On one occasion I (Ross) accompanied him to the bank. I watched several bank officers drop what they were doing to come over and greet Bill and ask if there was anything they could do for him. I was envious of the preferential treatment he received. I have my home mortgage with that bank, but none of the officers even knows my name.

Bill has everything money can buy — prestige and comfort. The only thing that Bill lacks is the one thing that money can't buy — happiness. His wife has given up trying to relate to him on anything but a surface level. He is lonely and often masks his hurt with alcohol. Once, after drinking, Bill came over to talk. He poured out a story of physical abuse and parental disapproval. His father was a real power broker. He remembers his dad's political wheeling and dealing. His dad had little time for the family. Bill and his sister were viewed as irritants, which needed to be removed. On one particularly difficult afternoon, Bill remembers his dad yelling at him, "You will never amount to anything!" Bill purposed to prove his dad wrong. He has been driven by this quest for success in search of his father's approval. Bill has paid a heavy price for his financial success. He has lost the intimacy of his wife and fellowship with God.

There was a time when Bill prayed, attended church, and sought God's will for his life. Since he is so financially prosperous, prayer is reduced to a social custom at meal time. Personal devotion has ceased and church attendance has continued only for image sake.

Those caught up in the struggle for approval will often be overly concerned about their image; that is, how they look, talk, act. Their image must conform to some illusion they have concocted, and the whole while they are further and further into the process of losing themselves. Anne Wilson Schaef, in her book *Codependency: Misunderstood, Mistreated* (Harper & Row, 1986), talks about how impression management (image) is part and parcel of codependency. It is the over concern of trying to become something you are not, with the ultimate loss of the self.

Christians are vulnerable to this dysfunction. It is so tempting to go to church with pious faces, looking our best. It is not fashionable to talk about our failures in our marriages, families, or businesses. It is not acceptable to discuss our struggles with greed, envy, and lust. We are tempted to conform to an image that we believe fits our idea of success. With this process, we bury our hurts and pains deeper and deeper inside. These become the fuel for our addictive and compulsive behaviors, and we lose touch with our true selves.

We need to slow down and think deeply about what is important. Is keeping up with the Joneses really that important? Are the external trappings necessary to make us feel better? Or is it time to redecorate our inner being with new spiritual values? We will explore the value and meaning of work as it relates to this topic in a future chapter.

Self-Exploration

● List several areas where you are concerned about what others think of you:

_____

_____

_____

_____

● Have you ever felt, "If they really knew me, they wouldn't like me"? Explain:

_____

_____

_____

● List several things that you don't like to do, but you do them because you "ought" to: _____

_____

_____

_____

● Are any of your "ought to's" because of what others might think if you didn't? Explain: _____

_____

_____

● What are the ingredients of a successful life?_____

_____

_____

● How would you define financial success?_____

_____

_____

Step Two Application

We came to believe that a power greater than ourselves could restore us to sanity.

"For it is God who works in you to will and to act according to His good purpose" (Philippians 2:13).

Susan and her two children were leaving. Ron had an impulse to reach out to his daughter and hug her, but held back. He hugged the grandchildren instead and said, "Good bye and good luck" to his daughter, after she was already backing out the driveway.

"Why didn't you hug Susan?" Ron's wife asked curiously.

"I don't know," he said.

Later as Ron was thinking about it, he came up with two possible reasons why he didn't show affection to his daughter. One was to punish her. She had hurt him terribly by running away in high school, becoming pregnant, getting married, and getting a divorce. She was guilty of flaunting the family values that Ron had believed in, and he was still holding it against her. The second possible reason why Ron wouldn't hug Susan was because he didn't want to get close to her, for fear she would hurt him again. If he kept his distance, she couldn't disappoint him or refuse to take his advice.

When Ron mentioned these possible reasons to his wife, she commented, "I think you are exactly right; that is the way you control all your relationships."

"What do you mean?" Ron asked defensively.

"Well, if you are going to get angry, I'm not going to tell you," she replied.

After several promises not to get angry and to listen without comment, Ron's wife let him have it. She said that affection, approval, and guilt were his main weapons to control all his relationships. In fact, these were the major tools he used with her. Whenever she didn't do exactly what he wanted, he would give her the cold shoulder and seek to make her feel guilty for failing as a wife. If she didn't agree with his politics, for example, he gave her the silent treatment. But if she served his favorite dinner on time, he was all "lovey dovey." She gave additional illustrations of his treatment of their other children; it wasn't just Susan.

Her final illustrations were from Ron's work. She explained how he used guilt motivation and withholding of approval as a means of manipulating his employees. Ron was good at making people feel guilty if they didn't meet up to his expectations.

All this was quite overwhelming to Ron. He had opened a crack of vulnerability in expressing his feelings about Susan, and in came a flood of condemnation. He was stunned at how aggressive his wife had become after he had given her permission to tell him whatever she wanted and promised not to get mad. He wished he hadn't made that promise, because inside he was furious. With great effort he kept it inside until the next men's Twelve Step group meeting. He virtually exploded with emotion and frustration as he told us his story that week. He felt completely undone and unable to handle the weight of feeling so helpless and hopeless. Our meeting went overtime as each man affirmed Ron and shared similar experiences in their lives. We concluded with prayers that recognized that only God, a power greater than ourselves, could restore us to sanity.

Once we see an area of powerlessness in our lives, it is like a floodgate opens up. Suddenly all these other areas pop up where we are just as powerless. As we become more and more aware of our powerlessness over the consequences of our compulsive behavior, we could easily lose hope. "Is there no way out?" we might ask. Where can we turn to gain some control in our lives? It is increasingly obvious that we can't manage things.

Thankfully, with God comes hope. In Step Two we continue the process of accepting our powerlessness to change the consequences in our lives. We come to recognize our need for God to enter in and transform our thinking and behavior. This is not easy to do. We are used to thinking that we are in control and can make things turn out our way. But now we are beginning to see that our attempts to manage our lives and our addictions have only made our lives more unmanageable. We now see that our overachieving, overworking, overcommiting, and overcontrolling have only added to the unmanageability.

Only when we've come to these realizations: (1) that we need power outside ourselves, (2) that we need guidance outside ourselves, and (3) that we need deliverance outside ourselves, do we see our need for God. Basically, our life's experience has driven us to the conclusion that we need Jesus Christ (a Savior, deliverance from outside ourselves); we need the Holy Spirit (power from outside ourselves); and we need the Scriptures (guidance from outside ourselves). With a firm commitment to Jesus Christ, His Word, and His Spirit, we are ready to look at those things which we have trusted in the past to relieve our pain and to give meaning to our lives.

As we let God enter our lives by yielding control to Him, we will need to honestly face those things that have previously occupied the place where God should have been. These things can include:
- Money
- Sex
- Chemicals
- Work
- Relationships

Anything that we have depended on to give meaning to our lives has knowingly or unknowingly been elevated to the status of being a god, by taking the place rightfully belonging to the only true God. It is hard to be honest about this. We must look at what we have given undue priority. What are the activities that have crowded out what we truly value?

As with any meaningful relationship, having a relationship with God will require time— time spent reading and meditating on His Word. God communicates with us primarily through His Word. There is no shortcut to relating to Him. If we will take the time to get to know Him, He will reveal Himself to us. He will walk with us and guide our daily steps. The Christian faith is very difficult and yet profoundly simple.

"But as many as received Him, to them He gave the right to become children of God, even to those who believe in His name" (John 1:12, NASB).

Believing in a power greater than ourselves (our God) requires faith. This faith is a faith in God, not faith in our own skills and strengths or some unfounded belief that "everything will work out in the end." That kind of faith is not enough to restore us to sanity. We must "let go" and trust God exclusively. If we trust God daily and seek His will for our lives by reading His Word, our faith will grow (Romans 10:17). We will realize that He is there for us. "I will never leave you nor forsake you" (Hebrews 13:5). All we have to do is to reach out to Him, and He will be there. It doesn't take a lot of faith, just faith in the right object—God (Mark 11:22).

"If you have faith as a mustard seed, you shall say to this mountain, 'Move from here to there,' and it shall move; and nothing shall be impossible for you" (Matthew 17:20b, NASB).

● Do you have any reason to believe that God can't be trusted? Explain:

_____

_____

_____

● Have you had an overwhelming experience of seeing your powerlessness in any area of your life? Briefly describe: _____

_____

_____

● Use a weather report to describe your relationship with God today (i.e., sunny and warm, partly cloudy, tornado warning) and explain why you answered as you did:

_____

_____

_____

"And whatever we ask we receive from Him, because we keep His commandments and do the things that are pleasing in His sight" (1 John 3:22, NASB).

"Jesus said to him, 'If you can believe, all things are possible to him who believes.' Immediately the father of the child cried out and said with tears, 'Lord, I believe; help my unbelief!' " (Mark 9:23-24, NKJV)

● What are the areas in your life that you need help to believe God for? Can you identify with the desperate father—"Help my unbelief!"?_____

_____

_____

_____

_____

_____

● What are some of the areas in your life where you find it difficult to trust:

Yourself?_____

_____

Others?_____

_____

God? _____

_____

Don't get discouraged by the fact that the road to recovery is never an easy one. We all would like instant success. Who wouldn't like God to reach down into our distress and perform a miracle? However, it is that kind of wishful thinking and escapism that has largely contributed to the situation we find ourselves in. That is because it violates the way God operates. God is interested in more than our relief and comfort; He is after character. When God doesn't rescue us immediately in answer to our prayers, we start doubting that He really cares. What is revealed, however, is our true character. The true nature of our character is not revealed in comfort, but in struggle. Our true inner emotional nature is revealed as we work through difficult situations. James 1:2-3 tells us to "count it all joy when you fall into various trials, knowing that the testing of your faith produces patience. But let patience have its perfect work, that you may be perfect and entire, lacking nothing." So we see that by properly dealing with our struggles, patience will be produced, which in turn matures our character.

● Can you think of some way that God might be using your current circumstances to teach you something? _____

_____

_____

_____

● How are denial and compulsive behavior used to avoid learning what God may be trying to teach? _____

_____

_____

_____

There are several steps along the road to trusting God which we can outline. They include:
1. We need to admit that we are in need, unable to manage our lives alone. We need a Savior, Jesus Christ.
2. We need to ask God for His help along the way.
3. We need to itemize the areas in which we specifically need God to help us.
Mostly, what we need to "work our programs" is courage and the patience to see the power of God at work in our lives. As we trust Him and endeavor to know Him day by day, we will see our lives changed.

"So do not fear, for I am with you; do not be dismayed, for I am your God. I will strengthen you and help you; I will uphold you with My righteous right hand" (Isaiah 41:10).

Professional Experience

As I (Dave) have worked with men over the years, I have seen again and again how hard it is for us to admit that we can't handle our problems alone. We are taught by our parents, friends, and the media that we can develop the ability to tackle anything that comes our way. It can be very hard to say, "I need some help!"

Even as a professional who encourages people to trust others, I have also found it difficult to reach out for help. Real or imagined, I feel the tension of trying to be self-reliant. It can be difficult to shake the feeling of weakness in admitting that something you have been trying to do is not working. Our culture seems to be saying to men: "Try as hard as you can and you can succeed at anything." The underlying message seems to be that of personal power and self-reliance. While this message is not entirely false, there are inherent problems when we buy into it wholesale. Is there too great a price tag for "success" as we have defined it? Is it time for us to re-evaluate our values and definition of success?

Recovery Affirmations

The goal of Step Two work combined with the issues raised in this chapter is to give up our belief that our own power and investment in image will gain us anything. Rather, we want to believe that God, and His rule over our lives, will give us the peace we seek. On a daily basis, for the next week, meditate on Psalm 91 and affirm that:

- God cares about me and will help restore me to well-being;

- He is powerful and has the answers I need for my life;

- I am already beginning to heal;

- With God's help I can make necessary changes in my life.

Prayer for Reliance on God

Dear God,

As You know, my life is out of control. I confess that I have been behaving in self-defeating ways. For many years now I have insisted that my way was always right. I now realize that that thinking is "crazy." Your Word points out that my way is right only in my own eyes. I confess my self-righteousness and crazy thinking as sin and thank You for Your forgiveness. I believe that You, God, can restore me to sanity. I pray now that You will enable me to let go of my need to always be right and learn to trust You.

In the name of the Lord Jesus Christ,

Amen.

Three

Men and Faith

Faith, as used in this chapter, is meant to mean religious faith. It is that fabric that holds life together. It sets the backdrop of meaning to the rest of life. It helps us understand ourselves, why things happen the way they do, and the purpose for all of life. Faith can answer the question, "Why am I here?"

For many men, there is little faith to our daily lives. We worship on a few Sundays a month, as long as it does not conflict with the sports schedule or our vocations. For most of us, our religious faith can never be said to take central priority in our lives. For most, God is only there when we need Him. As the old saying goes, "There are no atheists in foxholes."

When men are asked if they believe in God, they are quick to say yes. Why, then, is God not worth the time to really get to know Him? There is no easy answer to this question. Perhaps it goes back to what we know about how men are created. They were created to be warriors and producers. They want to be conquering something. This usually comes out in the competitive avenues of sports or their vocation. And, of course, this is not necessarily a negative thing. It is an aspect of our masculinity to be understood.

It is difficult, and goes against the natural grain, to value contemplation and solitude. Our society has never put a premium on inner reflection and quietness. These, however, are the disciplines needed to really get to know God. We cannot continue to leave these qualities to the theologians. To know God and have Him be an integral part of our daily lives, we must spend quiet time with Him—talking *and* listening. This will be an arduous endeavor, but very worthwhile. Richard Foster's book *The Celebration of Discipline* (Harper & Row, 1978) would be very worthwhile reading on this topic.

Let's look for a moment at a few of the disciplines which make up this faith, and which will give us many benefits if we will take the time to practice them.

Reading Scripture. It is our belief that God's Word, the Scriptures, is the primary way that God talks to us today. As we men move on in our emotional and spiritual journey, we need a Guide. By reading this workbook, you have decided that you need help outside of yourself. This is where the Scriptures come in. They are your personal roadmap by which you can navigate through life.

J.I. Packer, in a great book called *Knowing God* (InterVarsity Press, 1979), says that the Bible is to be read as a personal letter to each of His spiritual children. He adds that the Scriptures have the ability to expose many of our character defects, such as sinful habits, a tendency toward hypocrisy, natural self-righteousness and self-reliance, worldliness, and fearfulness. Additionally, this personal letter has the unique power to evoke joy, assurance, boldness, and liberty from those who love Him (*Knowing God*, p. 231).

Meditation. Meditation is the lost discipline of quietly listening to God. It includes reflecting on some aspect of God, such as His grace, or His marvelous creation. We suggest meditating on a portion of Scripture, such as John 1:1. We should take the time, every day, to spend fifteen minutes just thinking about God, and some aspect of His nature. We should think about what He is trying to say to us in our lives. Remember that He cares about us in a personal way and is "ordering our steps." Meditation, as with any new experience, is likely to be uncomfortable at first. With practice it becomes easier and very rewarding.

Prayer. This often neglected backbone of the spiritual life is essential to spiritual growth. Too often we think about prayer when we are in trouble. What we need to be doing is spending time each day talking to our Creator and listening to Him. It would be an excellent practice to start and finish each day reflecting on the first Three Steps, reading a portion of Scripture, and praying. A wonderful pattern for prayer, if you have none, is the following:

    A—Adoration: Praising God for who He is.
    C—Confession: Admitting your sins and asking God's forgiveness.
    T—Thanksgiving: Thanking Him for the many blessings you receive each day.
    S—Supplication: Asking Him to meet your needs.

Fasting. This is another of the Christian disciplines that is too often left to the "dyed-in-the-wool" believers. It can be used as a simple tool to increase focus on God and His work in our lives. A simple way to begin this discipline is to fast from sundown one day until dinner the next. The time between should be used to focus our attention on our relationship to God.

Dreams. Used cautiously, dreams can be another way to listen to the voice of God and get to know your inner self better as well. In both the Old and New Testaments, dreams and visions were regarded as another form of communication between God and humanity. Yet now, most of us hardly remember our dreams or take the effort to glean the valuable information contained in them. "As our spiritual friends, our dreams are constantly encouraging us to be open to a fresh word from God—sometimes a word of reassurance, at other times of warning, guidance, or command. Whatever they say to us, our dreams can render God's presence so vividly that our lives will never be the same" (Leroy T. Howe, "Dreams as Spiritual Friends," *Weavings,* July/August 1987, p. 39).

If you decide to try to expand this area of your personal life, we suggest that you take a few steps first. *One,* pray for receptivity to God's messages that might come through your dream life. *Second,* place a note pad or tape recorder next to your bed to note your dream immediately after awaking. *Third,* when you have time, note your associations to the dream. How did you feel in the dream? Were you active or passive in the dream? Also, remember, there is rarely a "right" interpretation to your dream. If you practice journaling your dreams, you will come to understand your dreams more effectively.

There are many other ways to develop spiritual health. We have listed only a few. The way to begin is to begin. God accepts us just where we are. He knows our hearts and our intentions and will honor them.

As we begin the process of communicating with, and listening to, God, keep in mind several foundational principles. J.I. Packer suggests the following:

1. God has spoken to man through the Bible;
2. God is Lord and King over His world, and seeks our worship of Him;
3. God, through the Lord Jesus, rescues us from guilt and the power of sin, and adopts us as sons;
4. Our God is a triune God: Father, Son, Holy Spirit;
5. Godliness means responding to God in trust, obedience, worship, prayer, and praise (*Knowing God*, pp. 15-16).

Getting to know God is like an exciting journey into an unknown land, filled with many new adventures. God bless you as you begin to know the greatest possible influence in your life. God will bless you as you seek to know Him.

"For the word of God is living and powerful, and sharper than any two-edged sword, piercing even to the division of soul and spirit, and of joints and marrow, and is a discerner of the thoughts and intents of the heart" (Hebrews 4:12, NKJV).

Self-Exploration

● What was the religious faith in your home during childhood? _____

_____

_____

● What is your attitude toward the Bible? Do you view it as a personal roadmap for your life? _____

_____

_____

_____

● Have you had any remarkable answers to prayer? _____

_____

_____

● What does meditation mean to you? Have you ever done it? _____

_____

_____

● How much time, per day, do you spend in quiet reflection or prayer?

None at all _____

5–15 minutes _____

15–30 minutes _____

More than 30 minutes _____

● If you were to get serious about setting time (or more time) aside for prayer and reflection, what would have to go from your schedule? _____

_____

_____

"So incline your ear to wisdom, and apply your heart to understanding; yes, if you cry out for discernment, and lift up your voice for understanding, if you seek her as silver, and search for her as for hidden treasures; then you will understand the fear of the Lord, and find the knowledge of God" (Proverbs 2:2-5).

● What does that verse about the wisdom of God mean to you?_____

_____

_____

_____

● What is your desire for your spiritual life?_____

_____

_____

_____

Step Three Application

We made a decision to turn our wills and our lives over to the care of God as we understood Him.

"Therefore, I urge you, brothers, in view of God's mercy, to offer your bodies as living sacrifices, holy and pleasing to God—which is your spiritual worship" (Romans 12:1).

Step Three, perhaps more than any other step, is a critical one to the recovering person. The previous steps have to do with attitudes and beliefs. It is one thing to acknowledge something; it is another thing, entirely, to make a decision based on those beliefs. So many of us have intellectually acknowledged a truth. We have known what is best to do, yet we have used denial for so long that we have lost the ability to be honest with ourselves. Now, in utter futility, we are finally ready to make a decision based on the hopelessness of our condition. We are now ready to turn our wills and our lives over to the care of God. Exactly how to do that is another matter. It is enough, for today, that we are making a crucial decision to look to God to manage our lives.

We have said before, and will say again, that the turning of our lives over to God is not a once-and-for-all event. It is a process. This means that we must daily ask God to manage our lives. Each day we must seek His will for us. Each day we must thank Him for all that comes to us, filtered through His loving hands, knowing that all is meant for our good (Romans 8:28). This will be very hard for most, since we are accustomed to trying to control life. We are tempted to blame ourselves for all failures and to keep working harder for perfection. Turning our lives over to God will not be easy.

What does "letting go" mean? We hear this phrase so often, but the balance between doing our part, yet trying not to be overly controlling, can be hard to find. Letting go means:

1. Caring, not caretaking;
2. Allowing others to learn from natural consequences;
3. Not judging others;
4. Focusing on ourselves, rather than others.

Trying to control all of life is an exhausting process. We have been compulsive in our own particular addictions. We have blocked out important parts of our lives in search of that one thing that would give us happiness. As a result, our lives have become unbalanced. There has been no rudder to guide our ship. We have been left to our own failing guidance system. Now we are beginning to see how far off course we have drifted. Fortunately, there is a Master Captain who will help us get back on course—Jesus Christ. And He has left for us a Master Chart to steer us on our way—the Bible.

● What are your greatest fears about turning your will and life over to God?

_____

_____

_____

● Do you have trouble believing that God has things under control? Why?

_____

_____

_____

● Reaching out to others, and trusting them, is very hard for most of us. Trust requires being vulnerable, being dependent on others. This has caused us pain some-where in our past. We still hold onto the wounds caused by that broken trust. List the significant times you can recall where someone you trusted let you down:

_____

_____

_____

● What are the feelings that you still harbor from that broken trust? _____

_____

_____

"Trust in the Lord with all your heart, and lean not on your own understanding; in all your ways acknowledge Him, and He shall direct your paths" (Proverbs 3:5-6, NKJV).

● What does Proverbs 3:5-6 mean to you? _____

_____

_____

Professional Experience

It is a frightening thing to recognize the extent of our maladies. It is no wonder we used denial for so long. Without the right attitude, our new insights can be overwhelm-ing. It is tempting to say again and again, "God, I'm doing the best I can." Or, "Please be patient with me. God is not finished with me yet." Perhaps the best motto for living is simply, "One day at a time."

Another aspect of recovery is learning that I don't have to have it all together. There is nothing shameful about needing help, whether we are professional people or blue-collar workers. We are all just human and can never expect to be more than what we are. I (Dave) have found in my own life, and in the lives of the men I work with, that it is difficult not to feel shame about not being able to manage our lives. But when I confront those old tapes in my head, I can slowly give myself a new message by which to operate.

Since the beginning of my own recovery process I have had an active prayer life and time of meditation. While it was awkward at first, I have come to rely on it more and more as an important part of my day. That time has helped me in "letting go" of areas that I cannot control, as well as obtaining inspiration from God about direction for my life.

Recovery Affirmations

Step Three has to do with our not playing God anymore in our lives. We have tried that for a long time, and it never works. While we are not at all sure about this new journey, nor of the One who is willing to lead us, we are willing to try this new path.

As we move along in this journey of "letting go," let's remember that He has the world in His hands. Deuteronomy 33:27 says:

"The eternal God is your refuge, and underneath are the everlasting arms."

Read this verse daily this week, and affirm that:

- God is in control of this world and my life;

- He cares about every detail of my life;

- I can "let go" and trust Him;

- He will give me guidance through His Word and prayer.

Prayer for Trusting God

Dear God,

There are so many ways that I try to control my circumstances and the people around me. Things never turn out the way I'd like, and then I'm discouraged. And people rarely do what I expect, and then I'm angry. Father, I want to "let go." I want to trust You to provide what is best for me, which You have promised if I listen to You. Thank You for caring about me.

Amen.

Four

Family of Origin, Marriage, and Intimacy

"My dad is smarter than your dad," Johnny was yelling to a neighborhood playmate. "And besides that, he has his own computer!" Well, now, that settles it, doesn't it! We smile at Johnny's bragging about his dad. In Johnny's eyes, no one is bigger, smarter, or more famous than his dad. Unfortunately, a child's unquestioned belief in his parents may eventually be the cause of some serious pain.

After all, our parents are just people. They are very human, and as such, make mistakes just as you and I do. But for a number of very critical years, they effect tremendous influence on us. Most child-development specialists believe that the first five years of life are critical for personality development, and if there is significant difficulty here, there will be profound difficulties for the child throughout life. John Bradshaw, author of the book *Bradshaw On: The Family,* says, "While it's always been known that our families influence us, we're now discovering that the influence is beyond what we've imagined" (Health Communications, p. 1).

Our parenting and, incidentally, our parents' parenting, greatly affects how we feel about ourselves. Most of us have core developmental issues and needs left over from childhood that we have never faced, but which continue to influence our daily lives. Now the point here is not to blame our parents. Blame is always counter-productive. The point is to face who we really are, how we have been negatively influenced, and to set about making necessary corrections. The good news is that we can parent ourselves again, this time knowing just what our needs are. And we have the help of the Holy Spirit who will guide us in the process.

One of the first steps needed, however, is to release ourselves from idealizing our parents. The trick is to develop a balanced perspective of them—neither too harsh, nor too naive. Many of us have used denial for many years, not wanting to look too closely at our birth order, the various traumas we may have experienced while growing up, or the effect our parents have had on us.

Bradshaw cites the following ways that parents may have hurt their children:
1. By physically abandoning them;
2. By not modeling their emotions for their children;
3. By not being there to affirm their children's expressions of emotions;
4. By not providing for their children's developmental dependency needs;
5. By physically, sexually, emotionally, or spiritually abusing them;
6. By using children to take care of their own unmet dependency needs;
7. By using children to take care of their marriages;
8. By hiding and denying their shame secrets to the outside world so that the children have to protect these covert issues in order to keep the family balance;
9. By not giving them their time, attention, and direction;
10. By acting shameless (*Bradshaw On: The Family*, p. 3).

This is quite a list! It covers most, if not all, of the ways a child can be harmed by well-intentioned parents. Most men do not think about these issues, so don't feel badly if you have not given them serious consideration. However, chances are good that you have been negatively influenced by some of them.

Roger had read the preceding list at a men's support group meeting, but nothing seemed to jump out at him. A few days later he woke in the middle of the night, and his wife wasn't beside him. He felt panicky, jumped out of bed, and ran through the house looking for her. He found her in the den and Roger asked angrily, "WHAT is going on?" She explained that she hadn't been able to sleep, so she decided to get up and write a few letters. Roger went back to bed, not fully understanding the strong current of feelings he was having. As he lay there thinking about it, he recognized a connection to a feeling he had when he was a young boy. His mother used to leave him in the car while she went grocery shopping. He never knew when she would come back, and each time he felt he would never see her again. It was a deep fear of being abandoned, and his tears were not enough to get his mother to take him with her.

When Roger reread Bradshaw's list at the next men's meeting, the first item jumped out at him this time! A little later you will have an opportunity to record hurtful experiences in your childhood. You might want to come back to this list to help stimulate your thinking.

We are now discovering that many abusive patterns are generational. That is, they are handed down from generation to generation. For example, if your grandfather was raised during trying times, as was common, and he learned to be a workaholic, chances are good that your father learned that behavior and then passed it down to you. We know that alcoholism has a strong hereditary component to it. Untreated sexual abuse in previous generations continues to affect offspring in negative ways. Perhaps these are some examples of what the Scriptures meant in Exodus 20:5: " . . . punishing the children for the sin of the fathers to the third and fourth generation." Clearly, many of our struggles have to do with poor choices of our parents and grandparents. Again, however, the point is not to lay blame; it is for understanding, and, ultimately, compassion for our parents and ourselves.

In order to truly move forward, we must not deny that we have been affected in some negative ways. Our culture makes it very hard for a man to admit that he still has pain. Most of us grew up with the proverbs, "Don't cry over spilled milk." "It's over with now and in the past. There's nothing that I can do about it now." These are ways to rationalize our pain, to try to stop the inner hurting. However, a pain denied is ultimately a pain intensified. It will take greater amounts of denial to keep the pain suppressed. That pain may also be channeled into self-destructive behaviors such as workaholism, alcoholism, sex addiction, or rage-aholism.

Claudia Black, in her book *It Will Never Happen to Me* (Ballantine, 1987), notes three rules of dysfunctional families. See if any of them fit your family of origin.

1. *Don't talk.* Don't share family secrets outside of the home. Let's pretend that everything is fine here. Don't get angry at one another in the family or talk about the real issues.

2. *Don't trust.* Don't rely on parents because they are not really there for you. Also, don't trust anyone outside the home.

3. *Don't feel.* There is no opportunity in a dysfunctional family to deal with painful feelings. No one wants to hear them. Others have enough problems of their own. So, feelings become frozen, denied, suppressed, buried.

● Do you identify with any of these rules? Which one(s)? _____

_____

● What did these rules look like in your family of origin? _____

_____

_____

● Do you see any of these rules in your family now? Which one(s)? _____

_____

_____

It is only after we identify these patterns that we can begin to change them. Understanding is power: power to see what is real; power to feel what we feel; power to want what we want and seek it.

Once we are willing to look at our past and the abuse which may have occurred, what are some helpful steps toward resolution? As you approach healing, remember that there are no quick fixes. We have all tried those and they only made things worse. We are all in process, being transformed into Christ's image. But along the path there are some helpful steps we can take.

First, don't be afraid to get professional help. A Christian pastor or therapist can be a very helpful addition to your own personal work. Getting past points of intense pain and denial takes a lot of support and technical assistance. Find a well-trained clinician with whom you can work.

Second, get support for yourself. Most men live in isolation. Though we may have many "friends," most men have painfully few people who really know them. Men typically have a great deal of difficulty reaching out for help. It's just not the "macho" thing to do. Therefore, we keep our pain and suffering to ourselves. The shame remains a secret and devastates our self-esteem. A Christian men's support group can be a marvelous way to meet some emotional needs. And, believe it or not, there are many men out there just waiting to be invited to share in a weekly group.

Third, start a journaling process. Every day make a note of what you are learning about yourself and your needs. Make a note about what you are feeling, thinking, and what you want. As you listen to yourself, you will come to understand what is missing in your life. It can also be helpful to keep track of your dreams. This is another area not explored by most men. Our dreams are rich sources of information about ourselves, though they must be interpreted cautiously.

Fourth, list out the abuse to which you have been subjected. Don't be afraid to say it the way it is. Then, tell either your therapist or your support group. You will undoubtedly have to talk about it a number of times to really get the feelings out. These people will help you put the abuse in perspective. Most survivors of abuse blame themselves at some level. As you label and discuss the pain, strive for owning your feelings about it. You will probably find grief as a result of your losses. Don't be afraid of your grief. Or, you may experience some numbing as a result of years of blocking out your feelings. As you practice listening to your feelings, they will grow and prove useful in your recovery.

Fifth, consider developing a new "family" if yours continues to be painful and destructive. While you cannot change the family into which you were raised, you can choose a new family for yourself. This family can be chosen on the basis of mutual respect and joy in each others' lives.

Finally, commit all of your pain and recovery process to the Lord. Every day, as you are in your prayer time, ask the Lord to show you new ways of healing and insights necessary for your recovery. Ask for help as you consider what kind of relationship to continue to have with your parents, if they are still living.

"In the same way, the Spirit helps us in our weakness. We do not know what we ought to pray for, but the Spirit Himself intercedes for us with groans that words cannot express. And He who searches our hearts knows the mind of the Spirit, because the Spirit intercedes for the saints in accordance with God's will" (Romans 8:26-27).

Self-Exploration

● Take a few moments and list some of the abusive traits that have been in your parents' history, such as physical, verbal, sexual, alcohol abuse. You may also want to note such destructive tendencies as workaholism, eating disorders, rage-aholism, or sexual problems.

Father's father: _____

_____

Father's mother: _____

_____

Mother's father: _____

_____

Mother's mother: _____

_____

Father: _____

_____

Mother: _____

_____

- List any abuse in your background: _____

_____

_____

- What has been your attitude about this abuse? Have you tended to minimize it or even deny it? _____

_____

_____

- What effect do you think it has had on your life? _____

_____

_____

Many people have found it helpful to create a *genogram* to be able to visualize some of the issues we have been discussing. A genogram is simply a schematic of our genealogy. Here is a list of symbols used in a genogram, followed by an example to show you how it works:

Male: ▢   Children: ◯ ▢

Female: ◯   Codependent: ⬭ C

Divorce: D⫽   Abandonment: ⬭ X

Surrogate Spouse: (⬭ dashed)   Miscarriage or Abortion: Ⓧ ▣X

Alcoholism: ⬭ AA

GENOGRAM EXAMPLE

Norm and Ann Jones married around the time of World War II, and had three children before they divorced. Both remarried, and Norm had another child by his second wife, Beth. That was Wes. Wes married Ginger and they now have two young girls.

In doing his genogram, Wes was interested in knowing if there was any drug or alcohol problems in his family of origin. He also was concerned about any child abuse, anger problems, infidelity, workaholism, or trouble with communication, fears, or secrets.

Here was his first attempt at doing a genogram:

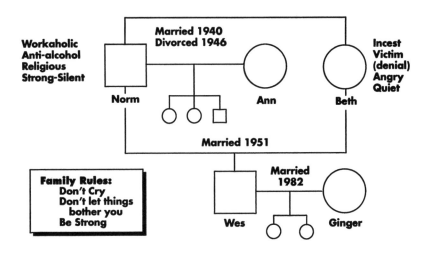

As a result of his "investigation," Wes found that his father, Norm, had struggled with workaholism, a learned trait from his own father. His father also had strong feelings and fears about alcohol because Wes' grandfather had a drinking problem. His father was the strong, silent type, not teaching the family how to share feelings. His mother, Beth, had survived "a little bit of wrong touching" by her father. Though she minimized it, it was hard not to miss the anger just below the surface. Much of Wes' parents' background was a secret to him because they did not readily share such information.

Using the symbols on page 50, draw out as best you can your grandparents, parents, siblings, and your own marriage(s) and children (there's space provided at the top of the next page). Write next to the particular people issues such as eating disorder, drug or alcohol addiction, workaholism, victimization or offender behaviors, etc. Make a note of any emotional problems of which you are aware.

MY GENOGRAM

● What new insights did you gain from this experience? _____

_____

_____

_____

● What are the "family secrets" that you weren't supposed to talk about?

_____

_____

Common Behaviors of Children from Dysfunctional Families

1. We have low self-esteem that causes us to judge ourselves and others without mercy.
2. We tend to isolate ourselves and to feel uneasy around other people, especially authority figures.

3. We are approval seekers and will do anything to make people like us.
4. We are intimidated by angry people and personal criticism.
5. We habitually choose to have relationships with emotionally unavailable people with addictive personalities.
6. We live life as victims and are attracted to other victims in our love and friendship relationships.
7. We are either super-responsible or super-irresponsible. We try to solve others' problems or expect others to solve our problems.
8. We feel guilty when we stand up for ourselves or act assertively.
9. We deny, minimize, or repress our feelings from our traumatic childhood.
10. We are dependent personalities who are terrified of rejection or abandonment. We tend to stay in jobs or relationships that are harmful to us.
11. Denial, isolation, control, and misplaced guilt are symptoms of family dysfunction. As a result of these behaviors, we feel hopeless and helpless.
12. We have difficulty with intimate relationships. We feel insecure and lack trust in others.
13. We have difficulty following projects through from beginning to end.
14. We have a strong need to be in control. We overreact to change over which we have no control.
15. We tend to be impulsive. We take action before considering alternative behaviors or possible consequences.

(Taken from *The Twelve Steps: A Spiritual Journey,* Recovery Publications, San Diego, California, 1988.)

● Which (if any) of the preceding symptoms fit you? _____

_____

_____

● Do you see any symptoms which you believe fit either of your parents?

_____

_____

_____

Men, Marriage, and Intimacy

If there is any area in which men are ill-equipped to handle the task facing them, we'd have to say it is being in an intimate relationship. While we have been somewhat prepared to look forward to marriage and being in a committed relationship, we have not been taught about intimacy.

Let's reflect for a moment on what is the goal and purpose of marriage. This is likely to be a question you have not considered before. God created us with the idea of marriage in mind. It was in His plan all along. Larry Crabb, in his book *The Marriage Builder* (Zondervan, 1982), says that God's purpose for us in marriage is to achieve:

1. The security of being truly loved and accepted;
2. The significance of making a substantial, lasting, positive impact on another person.

Marriage is the place where we can let our hair down, relax, and enjoy another caring for us in all of our situations. There is little that can compare to the feeling of being "in love" and having another's admiration of us. In that environment of acceptance, little can get us down.

Don sat quietly, reflecting on how wonderful the first few years with Jane had been. They had truly loved being together, and couldn't seem to get enough of each other's attention. Don marveled at some of the ways Jane did things. Her peculiarities seemed "cute" to him. She liked how he had a strong, tough exterior. Now, however, the joy was gone. The cuteness had shifted to annoyance. He hadn't really seen it slipping away. It was here one day and gone the next. "What am I going to do now?" he thought. "We can't put the magic back into our marriage."

The state of being "in love," in many ways, has little to do with achieving a quality, lasting relationship. Being "in love" does not necessarily mean that we know how to achieve intimacy with our partner. Most of us men are confused about what intimacy is and how we get and maintain it. We have never had adequate role models to learn how to develop intimacy and maintain relationships. It is little wonder that relationships haven't worked for us.

"What is intimacy, anyway?" was the question put to our men's group. "How will I know when I have it?" The long, awkward silence was surprising to all of us. With great difficulty we stumbled through the following list. Intimacy is:

"When you have trust."
"When you get appreciation from your partner."
"When you feel like you're in love."
"When you want to be with your partner."

While the list is true enough, it isn't complete. The list suggests that we men don't know what to look for, how to get it, or how to ask for it once we do define what we want. But as we look for answers, we will learn and get better at intimacy.

Janet Woititz, in her best-seller *Struggle for Intimacy,* says the following: "You know you are in a healthy, intimate relationship when you have created an environment where:

1. I can be me.
2. You can be you.
3. We can be us.
4. I can grow.
5. You can grow.
6. We can grow together" (Health Communications, pp. 20-21).

A healthy relationship is a dynamic, changing thing. It is not stagnant, any more than you or I should be stagnant and unchanging. Intimacy means that you have a relationship where you are accepted for the unique and wonderful person that you are. You do not have to be alike, or the way the other person would like you to be. Rather, you are valued for your "differentness."

Ray cried, "My wife has left me. She just up and left and refuses to talk to me." Our hearts went out to him. He was broken and in terrible pain. Over the next few weeks, Ray gained insight into his marriage. He admitted that he thought his wife was basically just like him—except physically of course. He thought she enjoyed fishing, hunting, and sports as much as he did. It was his wife's sister who told him that his wife had always hated those things and only did them because he insisted. Ray didn't have a clue as to what it was to be in an intimate relationship, but he was learning—the hard way.

To move toward warmth, growth, and intimacy, we must move away from judging each other, offering criticisms, and finding fault. We must move toward acceptance, affirmations, curiosity, and wonder. Marvel Harrison and Terry Kellogg say it like this:

> Intimacy is initiated and maintained in our ability to integrate the childlike wonder and noticing of another; the curiosity, trust and feeling of newness each day; the holding of hands, side by side watching the world and creation unfold, joining in the quest and questioning together, sharing the sparkle and eagerness of the forward movement of our lives. . . . When the childness and adulthood are integrated into our journey, the result is magical and respectful communion (*Changes,* October 1991, p. 53).

One more thought. Risk is the missing ingredient for many of us. We need to be willing to be vulnerable. We need to risk sharing our pain, needing our wives to be there for us, and us for them. And then recognize that there are no perfect relationships. Accept what your partner is able to give to you and you to her. If you will search for what you need, you will find it. Some will be given by your partner, some by others, and some by you giving in new ways to yourself.

Self-Exploration

- How were you prepared for marriage? Did you have premarital counseling?

_____

_____

- Where did you learn about sex? _____

_____

_____

- What is your definition of intimacy? _____

_____

_____

- What is your greatest disappointment in regards to marriage/intimate relationships?

_____

_____

_____

- What strengths to you think you bring to a relationship? _____

_____

_____

_____

_____

● What weaknesses do you think you bring to a relationship? _____

_____

_____

_____

● What are your hopes for your marriage? _____

_____

_____

_____

Step Four Application

We made a searching and fearless moral inventory of ourselves.

"Let us examine our ways and test them, and let us return to the Lord" (Lamentations 3:40).

OK. This is what much of the program hinges on: honesty with ourselves, and a willingness to see the "dark" side of our personality. You may be having one of two reactions. Perhaps you are saying, "No problem. I can do that. I've lived a pretty decent life, and I don't think there's anything too awful that I'm going to find." Or perhaps you join the ranks of those who look at this step and say, "Yikes! I don't like much of what I see. Why would I want to look further and deeper for more garbage?"

No one ever said that working a program of recovery didn't take courage and strength. The first scenario is often true for those who have not looked very hard into their defects. Denial is a strong force within all of us, in an attempt to protect ourselves. The second scenario fits those who have looked at themselves and have been humbled by what they have found. Courage is needed to proceed. But we must strive for the proper mindset as we undertake this work as well. The Scriptures remind us that: "Therefore, there is now no condemnation for those who are in Christ Jesus . . . " (Romans 8:1). Thank God we have been declared not guilty even though we fail Him on a daily basis. As we proceed to do our Fourth Step, we may feel convicted, but we are free from condemnation. We do not need to feel shame as we look at our shortcomings.

In this step we begin to really get to know our *self*. For most of us, we have been so busy focusing on other people, places, and situations, we no longer know who we are and what we think. Much of recovery hinges on us taking responsibility for ourselves. We now are ready to begin to give up the delusion that "if they would just quit . . . I'd be happy." Or, "It's all their fault that I'm. . . . " Learning not to blame others for our feelings and circumstances empowers us to make the necessary changes, so that our lives can be transformed the way God wants them to be.

"I've learned that doing a Fourth Step doesn't have to be frightening," said one woman at her Al-Anon meeting. "It all has to do with the way I approach the work. When I let myself see that this work is an ongoing process, it gets easier. I know that I will always have some 'housecleaning' to do, and I feel great after I take care of useless clutter in my life. I recommend it for everyone."

Approaching the Fourth Step

There are a variety of ways to approach Fourth Step work. The following is a method which may be useful to you, as recommended by Melody Beattie in her book *Codependents' Guide to the Twelve Steps* (Prentice-Hall, 1990). She recommends:

1. *Make an Inventory of Codependent Characteristics.* The behaviors to be focused on include caretaking; controlling; repressing feelings; not dealing with feelings appropriately; manipulation; self-neglect; not taking responsibility for ourselves; worrying; not liking and loving ourselves; not setting boundaries; not trusting God, to name a few issues.

2. *Write out a General Biographical Sketch,* focusing on who you are, and how you came to be who you are.

3. *Write out a Specific Biographical Sketch,* focusing on one area of your life, such as your history of relationships, family, or work history.

4. *Do a Big Book Fourth Step.* This approach is covered in the Big Book of Alcoholics Anonymous and asks us to take an inventory of those we resent, and why we resent them. We also list our fears and what we understand about them.

5. *List Things We've Done Wrong.* Here we look at what we've done to ourselves and others, that we feel guilty about. There will be areas where we feel appropriate guilt, and other areas where we feel inappropriate guilt. We may need some help in this area to sort out the difference.

6. *Explore and List the Wrongs Others Have Done to Us.* What people, institutions, places, and beliefs have victimized us? How did this affect our lives?

7. *Write out an Asset Inventory,* listing our good qualities, our talents, our values. It is often easy to see what is wrong with us, yet it can be difficult to focus on the positive.

8. *Finally, make a List of Anger, Fear, and Shame.* Here we write a list of all the people we are mad at, the things we are afraid of, and the things about ourselves which we try to hide. Go as far back as you can, and be as specific as possible. Let it all hang out. Remember, paper is cheap and you will receive lots of rewards from doing this work.

As you proceed with this courageous Fourth Step, remember to invite the Holy Spirit along to illuminate areas which need work, as well as areas which need healing. The Great Comforter would like nothing better than to help you heal past wounds.

Recovery Affirmations

The Fourth Step asks us to take a moral and fearless inventory. To do that, we need to affirm all that God has created us to be. He does not want us to live under a yoke of condemnation and guilt, or under a fear of others, but rather He wants us to examine our lives and look to Him for all our needs. This next week, meditate daily and affirm that:

- God will help us explore the truth about ourselves;

- He does not condemn us for who we were, are, or will become;

- All the feelings I find within are natural;

- I can change and grow, with God's help.

Fourth Step Prayer

Lord Jesus,

Help me to have courage in learning new things about myself, and in making the changes that You desire of me. Help me to let go of past hurts, places of victimization, resentments that I have held onto for years. May I live now in love, for myself, others, and Your creation.

Amen.

Five

Men, Friendships, and Support

Talk about awkward! The initial meeting of the men's therapy group was to start at 5:15. By 5:30, only two of the six men had arrived. These men nervously looked at one another and at the door, wondering what on earth they had gotten themselves into. As one of the therapists, I (Dave) wanted things to go well. Feeling very awkward myself, I wondered if this men's group was a good idea.

Our goal at the clinic had been to gather together a group of men with similar life situations, in hopes that they would relate to one another and eventually form a support group. Each of the men was in counseling and was encouraged by his respective therapist to attend.

Gradually, three other men reluctantly entered the room. By 5:45 five men were there, so we got started. To break the ice, I asked each of them to tell us the reasons why he had almost decided not to come. Each man felt that by coming to this group he was admitting that he had a problem. It was hard for them to admit they needed help. They each knew of others who were a lot worse off than they were. However, with some additional encouragement, mainly from their wives, they had reluctantly decided to come. Scared to death, but trying to look cool and calm, they entered an arena in which they had absolutely no experience.

Dean had a similar experience the night his girlfriend had left him. He desperately wanted to talk to someone, but who? His mind and heart raced. He wondered what was happening to him. He fumbled with the phone, trying to think of someone to call. What would he say? "Help"? "A lot of good that is going to do," he muttered to himself. In frustration, he hung up the phone. He remained alone in a world of pain and confusion.

We all know what's going on, don't we? It is our concept of manliness. It is simply not all right in our culture to reach out for help, let alone to cry out for it. That would be the ultimate sign of weakness. So we have to wait until our world literally collapses before we can say that something is not all right.

Sam Keen, in his best-seller about men, *Fire in the Belly* (Bantam, 1991), says that friendship among men "is an endangered species. Friendship doesn't thrive in a social ecology that stresses speed, constant preoccupation, and competition between men. . . . American men are homophobic, afraid of close friendships with other men. The moment we begin to feel warmly toward another man, the 'homosexual' panic button gets pushed" (p. 174).

The result of our fierce independent stance, according to Keen, is that men become overdependent on women to fill their need for intimacy. We then look to women around us to try to fill every possible need we have. Of course, that approach is doomed to failure, rendering men angry at themselves and at the women who are supposed to "be there for them."

The ignored truth is that we desperately need same-sex friendships to validate who we are and what we long to be. Sons need dads to model manhood. Little brothers need big brothers to emulate while growing up. Young men need other men to show them how to be men. Anything less inevitably leads us into that long, dark tunnel called isolation. In that tunnel we wear our masks, constantly pretending to be something, trying to be someone we think we should be, all the while not knowing who we truly are.

This dynamic is revealed in a common complaint that many wives have about their husbands. As one wife put it, "Chet only does it because I want him to; he doesn't do it on his own. He doesn't seem to have any convictions about it." The "it" in these sentences could be a number of things, like going to church, spending time with the kids, reading the Bible, or buying birthday cards for his parents. These men don't know their roles apart from the women in their lives. They need other men as close friends. In close friendship the layers are slowly peeled away.

There is reason for concern. Jim Fowles, in an article on the future of the American male, says that men are likely to become even more isolated in the '90s, according to attitudinal trends. He sees trends such as:

- a renewed ethic of achievement and independence;
- a greater self-orientation and less group-orientation;
- growth in attention to exercise and health, leading to a focus on self;
- more go-it-alone lives due to divorce and childlessness

("The American Male in 1990," *Futures Research Quarterly*, Fall 1985).

Perhaps the future is that bleak, or maybe we are tired enough of being alone. Maybe we are afraid enough of separation and divorce to do something different. Perhaps we are ready to look inside and make friends with ourselves and with each other.

"A man of many companions may come to ruin, but there is a friend who sticks closer than a brother" (Proverbs 18:24).

Self-Exploration

● Briefly describe the relationship you had with your dad while growing up. Break up your comments into the following time frames:

Ages 1–6 _____

_____

_____

Ages 7–13 _____

_____

_____

Ages 14–20 _____

_____

_____

Age 20+ _____

_____

_____

● Did you have a "best friend," a "buddy," while growing up? Describe your childhood friendships: _____

_____

_____

_____

● What are your current male friendships like? _____

_____

_____

_____

● Who would your wife say is a good male friend to you?_____

_____

● List three of your best friends and the kind of activities you do with them.

1. _____

2. _____

3. _____

● On a scale of 1–10, with 10 being very satisfying, rate how satisfied you are with your friendships.

      1   2   3   4   5   6   7   8   9   10

● What could you do to improve your friendships?_____

_____

_____

_____

● In what ways are you "real" with your friends? _____

_____

_____

● As men, we fill a variety of positions. We wear several "hats." List the "hats" that you wear:

1. Husband   2. Father

3. _____   4. _____

5. _____   6. _____

7. _____   8. _____

● In what ways do you play a role, or "wear a hat," to hide your true self?_____

_____

_____

Looking through Scripture for models which men could emulate, men appreciate King David as a man after God's own heart. Men can identify with David and his human struggles. Untold thousands of men have used Psalm 51 as an expression of their own repentance to God for their sins. However, there was one statement by David that confused me (Ross). The statement was one that David made concerning Jonathan in 2 Samuel 1:26. When David learned about King Saul's and Jonathan's deaths on the slopes of Mount Gilboa, he gave a very emotional lament (2 Samuel 1:19-27). In David's poetic expression of grief, he devotes the middle section exclusively to his feelings about Jonathan. It is here that David says, "How the mighty have fallen in battle! Jonathan lies slain on your heights. I grieve for you, Jonathan my brother; you were very dear to me. Your love for me was wonderful, more wonderful than that of women" (vv. 25-26).

My first reaction was, "No way!" How could a man's love for another man possibly be more wonderful than the love of a woman? I wanted to know. Most commentaries I consulted didn't even deal with the verse. Keil and Delitzsch in their commentary on 2 Samuel pointed out that the word *wonderful* has the additional meaning of being "distinguished." "Comparison to the love of woman is expressive of the deepest earnestness of devoted love" (*K & D*, Samuel, p. 292).

This statement of David's was an expression of his experience. Jonathan's distinguished devotion to David was greater than the devotion David had experienced from the women in his life. We have to remember that at the time David made this statement he had seven wives: (1) Michal, Saul's daughter (1 Samuel 18:27), (2) Ahinoam of Jezreel (1 Samuel 25:43), (3) Abigail, widow of Nabal (1 Samuel 25:43), (4) Maacah, daughter of Talmai (2 Samuel 4:3), (5) Haggith (2 Samuel 4:4), (6) Abital (2 Samuel 4:4), and (7) Eglah (2 Samuel 4:5). David's life experience until Saul's death was that of a fugitive in the wilderness. This did not lend itself to developing close relationships with his wives. As we know, it takes committed effort to develop a close relation to one wife, let alone seven! David found in Jonathan a devotion and kindred spirit that he didn't share with any of his wives. Examining the relationship of these two men will give us insights into developing our own friendships with men.

One reason David and Jonathan are said to have had a kindred spirit was because they both had singlehandedly done great exploits for God. David's defeat of Goliath is well known (1 Samuel 17). Jonathan's defeat of the Philistines (1 Samuel 14) is not as well known. Both faced impossible odds and with the help of God defeated the enemies of God. When they finally met, they shared similar zeal for God and His reputation. Their souls were "knit" (KJV) together. Today we call it "male bonding."

● What qualities of friendship do you find in the following verses:

1 Samuel 19:2-4 _____

_____

1 Samuel 20:41-42 _____

_____

1 Samuel 23:16-18 _____

_____

2 Samuel 9:1 _____

_____

2 Samuel 21:7 _____

_____

● In light of the principles of friendship we've been examining, what are two ways you could improve your man-to-man friendships?

1. _____

2. _____

Step Five Application

We admitted to God, to ourselves, and to another human being the exact nature of our wrongs.

"Therefore confess your sins to each other and pray for each other so that you may be healed" (James 5:16a).

In our home (Dave's), usually once during the spring, and again in the fall, my wife has a ritual which she goes through. She gathers up several boxes and proceeds upstairs. It is almost always on a Saturday afternoon when she has plenty of time. She proceeds to our walk-in closet, and there she does her sifting and sorting, deciding which clothes are to be part of her current wardrobe. The time is always one of laughter, surprises, reminiscing, and occasionally a wince of pain. She is doing what has become known as "spring cleaning." For her, things are never the same, and she does not want to be stuck with one way of dressing. At different times, during different phases of her life, she desires different looks. Everything is up for review.

Steps Four and Five are somewhat like this. We did Step Four to help us honestly look at ourselves. Remember, there is no right way of doing this, and you will probably want to do another Step Four next year, just to keep that closet from filling up with useless material. The foundation laid, now we are ready to quit pretending and reveal ourselves completely to another person. Who should that person be?

Step Five has three phases. The *first phase* is the most important and probably the easiest to do: admitting to God the exact nature of our wrongs. Ultimately, who can forgive sins but God alone? (Mark 2:7) It is to God that our offenses are directed. It is His moral law that we have broken (Psalm 51:4). God was the one who put us under the divine mandate to "love your neighbor as yourself." Therefore, to wrong our brother is first to break God's command. It is to God, then, that we must first admit our sins. God gives us a promise of forgiveness if we will admit to Him the exact nature of our wrongs. First John 1:9 says, "If we confess our sins, He is faithful and just to forgive us our sins and to cleanse us from all unrighteousness." To confess means to name the exact wrong committed. As we confess all the wrongs that we can remember, God will even forgive us for the offenses that we have already forgotten. That truth is contained in the second phrase by the words *all unrighteousness*. We could paraphrase the verse this way: "If we tell God the exact nature of the sins that we can remember, He is faithful and just to forgive us for the sins we can remember, and will remove the unrighteousness which is the result of the sins we've committed but don't remember."

Some have found it helpful to make a copy of their Searching Moral Inventory and to write on the top: TO GOD. They find a spot and a convenient time to be alone with God. They get down on their knees and read their moral inventory out loud to God, asking Him to forgive them for the things they've done wrong. When they have finished their confession, they burn the list. This visually reinforces the truth that these sins are now gone. As far as God is concerned, they are forgiven. However, there is an ongoing commitment that whenever one of these past sins surfaces to hinder or in some way bring back old behavior patterns, it will be dealt with on an ongoing basis. The ongoing character defects which are a result of personal sin will be dealt with in Steps Six and Seven, where we will be asking God to remove our defects of character and our shortcomings.

The *second phase* was actually started in Step Four. By writing out our Searching Moral Inventory, we were actually admitting to ourselves the exact nature of our wrongs.

The *third phase* is by far the most difficult to do: admitting to another person the exact nature of our wrongs. Choosing the person to whom you will reveal your "dark side," your soul, your very personhood, should not be a quick choice. It deserves a lot of attention and prayer. You will want to choose a person who has had experience listening to others and, perhaps, even listening to Fifth Steps. You will want your person to be nonjudgmental and compassionate. This is not a time to receive a lecture on all the things that you've done wrong. It should also be a person who will encourage you and affirm your strengths. After all, the program calls for a moral inventory, meaning an inventory of our behaviors according to our moral values. You will want to share the times you adhered to your values as well as those times when you didn't.

Another word about the person with whom you will choose to share your Fourth Step work. "The Twelve Step program" has a really nifty idea not found elsewhere, to our knowledge. The idea is a sponsor, or mentor. Ernie Larsen, in his great little book on the program called *Stage II Recovery,* says that we all need "someone special, who is chosen very carefully, who we trust, who has no need to elevate us or put us down, and who is farther along the road we're trying to travel. Such people have something to give us and we need to meet and talk with them regularly" (Harper San Francisco, 1985, pp. 70-71). Finally, as people who believe in the power of Jesus Christ, it will be important that you find someone who shares that commitment, so as not to guide you in wrong directions.

"So then, each of us will give an account of himself to God" (Romans 14:12).

● Write out your paraphrase of 1 John 1:9: _____

_____

_____

● What steps have you taken to gain God's forgiveness? _____

_____

_____

● Write out your paraphrase of James 5:16: _____

_____

_____

- How do you feel about sharing the exact nature of your wrongs with another person?

_____

_____

- Who is a person that you can trust with your inventory? _____

_____

Professional Experience

Recovery is based on giving up the notion that we only have ourselves to rely on. Now we have God and others to whom we can turn. Thankfully, there are many sources of help available to us. The risk that we take in reaching out to others will be repaid many times by the comfort we find in sharing our stories with others.

In addition to finding another person with whom to share our inventories—hopefully finding a mentor or sponsor in the process—we also will be richly blessed if we find a group with whom to be involved. Group involvement is really essential, but is something that will be stretching to most of us. We know how to play and compete in a group; sharing our souls in a group is another story. Yet the results are incredibly rewarding. Individuals can only give what they have to give. A group, however, has collective energy and strength. A team has more pulling power than an individual. When we are down, someone will be there to lift us up. It is in a group that we share our "experience, strength, and hope."

"Two are better than one, because they have a good return for their work: If one falls down, his friend can help him up. But pity the man who falls and has no one to help him up! Also, if two lie down together, they will keep warm. But how can one keep warm alone? A cord of three strands is not quickly broken" (Ecclesiastes 4:9-12).

Recovery Affirmations

There is something wonderful and hopeful that happens when we dare to gather together. The Gospel tells us that we need each other and are to share our needs and hope with one another. As we gather in Christ's name, we become more aware of our previous isolation, and we are given the opportunity to be reconciled to God and to one another. This is a tremendously healing experience.

As you consider finding a safe place where you can meet with other men, remember the words Christ spoke:

"Again, I tell you that if two of you on earth agree about anything you ask for, it will be done for you by My father in heaven. For where two or three come together in My name, there am I with them" (Matthew 18:19-20).

Remember these words this week and affirm:

- There is benefit for me when I gather with others;

- Christ will be there with me;

- Others are struggling with some of the same issues;

- I am capable of caring deeply for others.

Prayer for Support

Dear Lord,

You know that I am a lone ranger. I am not used to sharing my feelings with anyone. This is very hard for me. Yet I know you are telling me that I need to reach out to others.

Please help me to find just the right person with whom to share my Fifth Step and the right group where I can belong.

Amen.

Six

The Working Man

There was no place that Steve could go to escape Karen. She stayed right on his heels. "What is the matter with you? You're always mad. You're not interested in what's happening around this house. You haven't been to one of Stevie's games in two months." To get her off his back, Steve shouted, "Look, I've had four hours of sleep and have to go back to the plant at 6 o'clock tonight. Can't you just let me have a few hours of relaxation without always yapping at me?"

Such was the stalemate. Shift work went with living in a mill town. Steve was always tired from the rotating shifts. His job at the mill was routine and boring. He found little satisfaction in his work apart from the steady income that was needed to support his growing family. Finances were such that he had to work at least ten hours of overtime per week to get the bills paid and to keep the rest of the crew off his back. Because of Karen's nagging he had been bidding out to try to get straight days at work, but knew that if he ever had enough seniority to actually get it, his paycheck would suffer.

Karen had her own side of the story. It was just about impossible to have any kind of family life when her husband worked such crazy hours. The overtime only added to the confusion. She really wanted him to have a "normal" job, whatever that was, and be there with her and the children. Yet she was also painfully aware that they needed the extra money that he earned working overtime. "HELP!"

Kyle's story was quite different, but with similar effects. He was a man who had determined early that he would be "fulfilled," earn lots of money, and have all the nice things this world had to offer. He went to college, then graduate school, before ever seriously considering having a family. He married shortly before graduate school, but put off kids until the time was right. After completing his law degree, he joined a law firm and began the long, arduous ascent to the top. During the early years everything went perfectly: good money with lots of extra "bennies." His wife, Jill, was also enamored with the "good life." A few years later they began their family, and that also went just about as planned.

Problems started to surface about ten years later. They were living in the fast lane.

Eventually, Jill began to resent Kyle staying at the office until 8 or 9 weekday nights. Saturdays were no longer days off, but an extension of the work week. In fact, very little time really was preserved for the family. Kyle felt such a push to make his mark within the law firm, trying to get that partnership which eventually did come. Success has its price. With the partnership came even greater expectations of him, which in turn increased the resentments within the family.

Do you see any similarities in these two situations? What are the differences? In the first, the couple had to struggle to make a living. Steve was unfulfilled and always exhausted. Tension filled their marriage. Karen was getting the leftovers and not liking it. In the second scenario, Kyle was fulfilled in his rise to the top, but Jill complained that all she got were the leftovers.

The similarities are many and could be explored a great deal. One similarity is the focus on finances. Both families were preoccupied with money and material things. This material focus can lead to destructive results. Tom Eisenman, in his book *Temptations Men Face,* says that "Once our love of money elevates it to this supreme position in our lives, evil will naturally result. We lose all perspective. The power of the world captures us. Nothing will stand in our way—not friends, not family, not God" (InterVarsity Press, p. 137).

The Scriptures tell us not that money is the root of all evil, but the *love* of money is the root of all kinds of evil (1 Timothy 6:10). It is when we become preoccupied with attaining and keeping money that we lose perspective. And of course, work is the way most of us earn that money, hence, work takes on an inappropriate importance.

Another similarity in the stories was the loss of balance. Unfortunately, both men placed their work above the needs of their families, perhaps unknowingly at first. It is truly tragic that it takes a breakdown of some sort for us to see how out of balance our lives have become. It may take a spouse walking out the door before we see how much we have neglected our family life.

Yet another similarity is that neither man spent time truly enjoying his work. While Steve trudged through every day, clearly resenting the time he had to put in on the job, Kyle seemed to be enjoying his work. However, what was subtly occurring with Kyle was an obsession with earning money, power, and prestige. These commodities taste good going down, if you will, but are not nurturing. In other words, it would be just a matter of time before Kyle began to feel empty inside with the push to get to the top.

Bill Hybels, in his book *Honest to God,* states that there are two keys to maintaining a balance in your work and really enjoying your work. First, we must have "vocational authenticity, which means having the right job, for the right reason, and enjoy the right rewards" (Zondervan, p. 137). In other words, we must find a job that suits our personality. Steve clearly did not like his job, and may very well not have been suited for it. We know that God gifts us with varying abilities and talents and that there is a job out there for which we are suited.

The second requirement for an authentic job life, according to Hybels, is doing our work for the right reason. Now, if you are like us, you haven't given that one a whole lot of thought. Hybels states that the right reason is "to please and glorify God." Colossians 3:23-24 says, "Whatever you do, work at it with all your heart, as working for the Lord, not for men, since you know that you will receive an inheritance from the Lord as a reward. It is the Lord Christ you are serving."

We would all do well to be in prayer about our jobs, praying specifically that God would help us to understand our natures, talents, and God-given inclinations. Then we need to pray that we would keep in mind who our real Boss is, and that we will see the mission field wherever we are.

Work and Worth

As Sam Keen explains in *Fire in the Belly* (Bantam, p. 51), "Preparations for the male ritual of work began even before the age of schooling. Long before a boy child has a concept of the day after tomorrow, he will be asked by well-meaning but unconscious adults, 'What do you want to be when you grow up?' " The stage then becomes set to socialize young boys into the men's world of work. The message becomes clear that work is to be the center of his world.

Later, as adults, men will often greet one another, asking what they do for a living. Each will size the other up, often competitively, with occupation and income in mind. It is not hard to see how work can become all-consuming and take on more importance than being a good provider for the family. A man can easily buy into the notion that self-worth has to do with rank in the company, income level, and status of profession. And unfortunately, as soon as he does that, he will have sold his soul for that which cannot truly satisfy.

There is a minister in our town who illustrates this problem. Whenever he signs his name, he simply signs "Pastor." Whenever he introduces himself, he calls himself "Pastor." It appears that he has confused who he is with what he does. His identity is wrapped up in his job description. A man's occupation is a means to an end, not the end in itself. Our identity transcends what we do to who we are before God.

Society says: "It's the cost of the toys that separates the men from the boys." The Bible says, "Watch out! Be on your guard against all kinds of greed; a man's life does not consist in the abundance of his possessions" (Luke 12:15). The Apostle Paul knew what it was to have plenty and what it was to suffer want. About that he said, "I have learned to be content in whatever circumstances I am in" (Philippians 4:11).

In Paul's first letter to Timothy, he writes concerning the same concept of contentment. Read 1 Timothy 6:5-10 and answer the following questions:

● What does Paul say constitutes "great gain"?_____

_____

● With what are we to be content?_____

_____

● What happens to people who are eager for money? _____

_____

_____

As mentioned earlier, another pit we can fall into is comparing ourselves with another's accomplishments and possessions. There is an ad on TV in which a couple is looking out their kitchen window as they see a large yacht being pulled into their neighbor's driveway. They look at each other and ask, "Where did they get the money to do that?" Their envy is obvious. As Christians we know that envy and covetousness is wrong. After all, the Tenth Commandment states: "You shall not covet your neighbor's house. You shall not covet your neighbor's wife, or his manservant or maidservant, his ox or donkey, or anything that belongs to your neighbor" (Exodus 20:17).

However, I (Ross) thought I had found a way around that. You see, I don't want my neighbor's car, boat, or cam-corder. I simply want one just like it! With that little bit of semantic footwork I can still want what my neighbor has, without coveting. My guilt-free desires lasted only until I did a study on the works of the flesh. There is a pesky word in the King James Version called *emulation*, or *jealousy* in the New International Version. The word is defined as, "The desire created by the spectacle of another's possessions." My little scheme is undone.

● What does Paul say in 2 Corinthians 10:12 about those who compare themselves among themselves? _____

_____

_____

● Do you identify with either Steve or Kyle's stories? Explain: _____

_____

_____

● Under what sort of financial pressures do you find yourself? _____

_____

_____

● List several items you would like to have that are "just like" things your neighbor has: _____

_____

Workaholism

As we learn more about addictions, we find that even positive and creative activities, such as exercise and work, can become addicting. While work addiction is probably the most accepted and encouraged of all the addictions, it still can destroy and eventually kill a relationship. This flies in the face of all our traditional values, which told us, "If it's not worth doing right, it's not worth doing at all. Give 110 percent to everything you do."

In spite of society's constant encouragement to do more and more, climb higher and higher, workaholics are terribly unhappy people on the inside. According to Bryan Robinson, foremost expert on work addictions, workaholics are living in misery and despair despite the outward appearance and trappings of success. "Work abusers often give the excuse that they overindulge in work to provide for their families. But the truth is that the addicted overdo to fill an inner void. Excessive work medicates emotional pain and helps repress rage, fear, guilt, sadness, and an array of other emotions" (*Changes*, 1990, p. 56).

As with any addiction, those addicted will give lots of excuses, reasons, and explanations for their behavior. They may tell you that they would love to slow down if it were possible. The rationalizations abound. As we've said, slowing down may only occur when we "hit bottom."

● Here is a sampling of questions, adapted from Workaholics Anonymous, to help us determine the presence of work addiction in our lives:

1. Do you work more than forty hours per week?_____

2. Do you take your work home with you? On weekends? On vacation? _____

_____

3. Do you believe it is OK to work long hours if you love what you are doing?
Explain: _____

_____

_____

4. Are you afraid that if you don't work hard you will lose your job or be a failure?

Explain: _____

_____

_____

5. Do you do things energetically, including play? _____

_____

● By answering those questions, did you learn anything new about yourself? What?

_____

_____

_____

Ideas for Personal Recovery

Bryan Robinson suggests the following ideas for recovery, from his book entitled *Work Addiction* (Health Communications, 1989):

- Slow down your pace.
- Work in moderation.
- Strengthen family ties.
- Get back in the social swing.

- Learn to relax.
- Improve family climate.
- Celebrate life's rituals.
- Live in the now.

- Build social networks outside of work.
- Pamper yourself.
- Validate yourself.
- Seek spiritual healing.

- Develop social pastimes.
- Eat properly, rest, and exercise.
- Mourn the loss of your childhood.
- Attend a Twelve Step program.

- Which of these suggestions would you like to implement into your lifestyle?

_____

_____

_____

_____

God's View of Work

Jesus had a lot to say concerning our attitudes about work. It was Jesus who asked how smart it was to "gain the whole world but lose [your] soul!" Workaholism, in many ways, can be an attempt to have it all—the whole world. Insidiously, in the process, something changes: men neglect their family, their health, their relationship with Jesus Christ.

But we must be cautious not to let the pendulum swing to the other extreme. There is a scriptural basis for work. Since the beginning of time, God ordained that we should work for our livelihood. In Genesis 2:15 (NASB) we read, "Then the Lord God took the man and put him into the garden of Eden to cultivate it and keep it." The very first thing that God gave man to do was work.

But God also set some healthy parameters around work. He said, "You shall work six days, but on the seventh day you shall rest; even during plowing time and harvest you shall rest" (Exodus 34:21, NASB). This has been a hard principle for American culture to follow. We place such an emphasis on productivity. Rest and recreation are not valued by many.

The New Testament also gives many guidelines regarding work. Clearly the principle is that all are to be involved in some aspect of caring for ourselves and our families. "But if anyone does not provide for his own, and especially for those of his household, he has denied the faith, and is worse than an unbeliever" (1 Timothy 5:8, NASB).

The Scriptures tell us that we are to make excellence our standard at work. In many ways we present Christ to the world in all that we do and say. Our attitude toward work, and the way we perform it, says a lot about us. First Thessalonians 4:11-12 (NASB) says, "Make it your ambition to lead a quiet life and attend to your own business and work with your hands, just as we commanded you; so that you may behave properly toward outsiders and not be in any need." Jerry and Mary White, in their book which explores the purpose of work, believe that we are to work to:

- glorify God;
- provide for our family's needs;
- present a good reputation to the world (*On the Job*, NavPress, 1988).

Therefore, we must all strive to have a godly attitude toward work. This means seeing work through God's eyes. That means seeing our work as an avenue where we can be a witness for God and provide for our families' needs. If we idolize our work, that is, place it at the center of our lives, and let it define who we are and how we feel about ourselves, we will be disappointed. Idols are powerless and cannot help us when we experience true need. All the money, prestige, toys, and power will not help us at all in a time of despair.

Doug Sherman and William Hendricks say it well. "Loving God. Loving others. Loving ourselves. This is what God has told us to do. This is what he wants us to concentrate on. And our work, far from being opposed to these commands, is actually one of our most important means of fulfilling them. Work matters to God" (*Your Work Matters to God*, NavPress, 1987, p. 94).

Self-Exploration

- How do you feel about your work? _____

_____

_____

_____

- Do you see your identity tied up with your profession? Why or why not?

_____

_____

_____

● How would you feel and what would you do if you lost your job today?

_____

_____

_____

● If you could choose another profession, what would it be and why?

_____

_____

_____

● What opportunities do you have to be a witness for the Lord at your job?

_____

_____

_____

● What would you like to change about your job? _____

_____

_____

_____

Step Six Application

We were entirely ready to have God remove all these defects of character.

"Humble yourselves before the Lord, and He will lift you up" (James 4:10).

The prescription read, "Take until entire bottle is empty." The problem was that Mike was feeling better and he felt like *he* could handle things now. It was good to have the doctor there when he was in critical pain, and the prescription helped, but that was some time ago, and now he was ready to go it on his own.

Working a Twelve Step program can be much like this. We see the need for help when in serious pain and, reluctantly, are willing to reach out for help. But when we no longer are in serious need, a voice awakens inside of us which says, "Do it on your own." This voice will hurt us and is very self-destructive. We must continue to take the medications which have been helpful so far. We must trust this program to carry us to where we need to be. And trust is hard for us.

With addictions and dysfunctional behaviors, it takes a long time to get to the point where we are "entirely ready" to give up our self-destructive behaviors. While part of us wants to let them go, another part clings to them desperately. That is normal and very human. We must respect the power of our habits and patterns to continue exerting their influence over our lives.

And that is where the next step fits in. Having practiced turning our wills and lives over to the care of God, and having done some work on taking our inventories so that we can recognize our destructive patterns, we are now "ready" to have God remove these character defects. Remember, just the process of naming our character defects and "turning them over to God" is a powerful step toward changing. You are further down the road of change than you think.

" 'For I know the plans I have for you,' declares the Lord, 'plans to prosper you and not to harm you, plans to give you hope and a future' " (Jeremiah 29:11).

"Defects of character! Yuk! I hate the thought of having these defects of character!" Ted wrestled within himself as he thought about last night's men's support group meeting where Step Six was discussed. Oh, he knew he had problems, but "defects of character"? This seemed to be overstating the problem a little, didn't it?

Ted, like most of us, has a lot invested in seeing himself as basically a good person who has a few rough spots, but nothing needing remodeling. Touch-up paint would do well to make for good appearances. And we can see how others surely need this kind of program. Now we know that touch-up paint will not cover up the faults we see in *them*. Is it also possible that *we* have too much invested in covering up our problems? Is it possible that we might be threatened by what we would see if we looked honestly in the mirror? Why is it so hard to admit that we all have areas that need restoration?

The truth is, we have been created in love; we are unique creatures "in the image of God." Yet we have also been affected by the Fall and this invades every aspect of our lives. We are all wounded people who do not need to be condemned, but loved. When we truly love ourselves, we will find ourselves ready to face our weaknesses, knowing this is not reason for shame, but for compassion. We will grow, finding ourselves ready to give up:

- Self-hate
- Overwork
- Judgmentalism
- Guilt
- Control
- Fears

And we will begin to notice *and* accept:

- Limitations
- Needs
- Weaknesses in others
- Inward longing to be close to God

Accepting our character defects is so freeing. We then can quit hiding and open ourselves to the love of others and Abba Father too. We can quit trying so hard to make sure others don't see our weaknesses. In fact, for a while we might talk openly about them to those close to us. As we talk about them, we are already taking away some of the power they hold over us.

We would like to say a word about courage. Yes, the word we usually use to describe someone who can climb a mountain, kill a bear, or some other "manly thing." We fully believe it takes that same courage to look inside and face our past, to see who we are and how we came to be who we are. We believe we need to feel a sense of accomplishment at being willing to "go where few have gone before": the journey within!

- Do you feel ready to have God remove your character defects? Why or why not?

_____

- What are your fears as you approach this step? _____

_____

_____

_____

- If God had complete control of your life, what would He change? _____

_____

_____

_____

● If you feel courageous, ask someone who knows you well: "If God had complete control of my life, what do you think he would change?" _____

_____

_____

_____

"Do not conform any longer to the pattern of this world, but be transformed by the renewing of your mind. Then you will be able to test and approve what God's will is—His good, pleasing, and perfect will" (Romans 12:2).

"Therefore if any man be in Christ, he is a new creature; old things are passed away; behold, all things are become new" (2 Corinthians 5:17, KJV).

● As you renew your mind, describe the things that you are beginning to see change. How are you different from the "old you"?_____

_____

_____

_____

Professional Experience

This is probably the step which will indicate whether you are going to "stay with the course." Unfortunately, in my (Dave's) counseling practice, I see so many who begin to get better and then decide to do the rest on their own. Most who leave counseling prematurely do not make the changes they had hoped they would make. This is especially true of men, who have so many external and internal pressures to "get it together."

It is difficult to stay with something. In a time of "the quick fix," we all wish progress would happen faster. Yet that is not the way God created us. We must recognize how long these destructive patterns have been in place and then have respect for the fact that it may take as long to reverse those same patterns. Yet the journey of recovery can be terribly exciting.

So have respect for the challenge of change, and stay on course!

Recovery Affirmations

Step Six asks us to decide again and again to ready ourselves for the removal of our character defects. We are not the One who removes them. It is God's work to do that. It is our work to ready ourselves.

This next week, on a daily basis, affirm that:

- I am ready for God to reveal my character defects;

- God is already at work changing me;

- The "new me" will be better yet;

- God will give me the courage to change.

Sixth Step Prayer

Dear Lord,

I find that when I try to change, I fail. I want to rely on You to change me, in Your own time, in Your own way. I just want to be ready to be changed. Thank You for the promise that You will be with me in all my circumstances.

Amen.

Seven

Men, Morality, Ethics, and Integrity

We thought long and hard about whether or not this topic needed to be included in this workbook. After all, those of you reading this book don't exactly make a habit out of robbing banks and stealing old ladies' purses, do you?

Maybe you have cheated on your income taxes a time or two, but then again, who hasn't? And you know that even that is wrong, and you've probably vowed to give that up with your New Year's resolution. So what in the world is the problem? What does the word *ethics* even mean?

The dictionary definition is "a principle of right or good behavior" (*Webster's II, New Riverside University Dictionary*, Houghton Mifflin, 1984, p. 445). That helpful description reminded us of why we think the topic is worth being considered in our workbook. We men need to return to thinking about "right and good behavior."

Another word in our title for this chapter deserves some explanation as well. That word is *integrity*. This word, too, has to do with "character," that is, living according to a set of standards that will build up all involved. Obviously, this is very different from the exploitative nature that pervades our society. We will have trouble having integrity and a "get them before they get you" attitude at the same time. We will have trouble maintaining integrity if we look around us and base our actions on what others are doing. No, our standards, or ethics, will need to come from some other source if we are to rise above the level which we see around us.

Most of us have heard of "situational ethics"—perhaps we have even unknowingly practiced them. This essentially means that we adjust our ethics to fit each situation. "There are no absolutes," many will say. If there are no absolutes, then it follows that, "I will decide what is right and wrong for me for any given situation. I am measured by my own standards." This kind of thinking—that no value is stable and no truth is authoritative—destroys integrity and congruity. Thus, "Every man does what is right in his own eyes" (Judges 17:6).

The decadence that resulted in Israel when everyone did what was right in his own eyes is well documented in the Book of Judges. The degeneration of our society is likewise well documented. Our newspapers are filled, on a daily basis, with another scandal which signifies the further collapse of integrity. We have scandals in government, on Wall Street, even in the church. There is no arena free from the ravages of sin, which is the ultimate destroyer of integrity. What has been your reaction to the moral collapse of our nation? Do you find yourself saddened and sick at heart? Or, do you find yourself numbed, and tired of hearing of the latest scandal? Remember, we are all fundamentally the same, that is, lacking integrity in our hearts. We all need an inner change, not just an alteration of our outward appearances and behaviors, but a change of values and standards.

Jesus made it clear that integrity involves the whole of the inner person: heart, mind, and will. Warren Wiersbe, in his book *The Integrity Crisis,* states: "The person with integrity has a single heart. He doesn't try to love God and the world at the same time. His heart is in heaven and that's where his treasure is. . . . The person with integrity has a single mind, a single outlook that keeps life going in the right direction . . . the person with integrity has a single will; he seeks to serve but one master" (Oliver-Nelson, p. 22).

Crossing the Lines

When my (Dave's) son was young, my wife and I used to applaud any effort he would make at drawing. Any scribble on the page was considered a work of art equivalent to the Mona Lisa. We were sure he was a budding artist, though we have since reconsidered that opinion. Back then we considered any drawing outside the lines to be a sign of creativity; he was not to be hemmed in by convention.

As the years went by our attitude shifted, and we started to expect more conformity to the "lines." We began to give him the standard guidelines, boundaries if you will, that were originally created by God to help us, not hem us in. While we all want to do things our way, we need to seek the wisdom of our parents and God if we want true peace in our lives. Those who mature know the wisdom of obeying guidelines that have been established with our welfare in mind. The mature incorporate those boundaries internally, so they don't have to be "policed" by external boundaries. However, most of us, at one time or another, test this out to see if we really have to obey the rules. The lesson is tough to learn.

It was especially difficult for Karl to learn. He had been a successful realtor for over ten years. He had also been a man of discipline. He expected high standards of himself and of those around him. He never really considered the option of cheating to get ahead. Then temptation snuck up on him.

As he looks back at his "stepping across the line," he shakes his head and says, "I don't fully understand how I could have accepted those kickbacks. My reasons now appear so foolish." Karl has spent hours of self-analysis and has found many factors that contributed to his fall. It was partially due to increased business pressures. His more than occasional use of alcohol was a major factor. Certainly the pressure he felt to "keep up with" his colleagues was an issue. He really enjoyed all the extras he began to buy with the new income power. Regardless, he did not see the decline begin. He only saw it end, painfully.

Karl put the pieces of his life back together because he found help, sought to improve his relationship with God, and strengthened the "weak links" in his character. His story is ending well, but sometimes the story ends in tragedy. Temptation, more temptation, vulnerability, then . . . collapse. Coloring outside the lines.

"Do not love the world, nor the things in the world. If anyone loves the world, the love of the Father is not in him" (1 John 2:15).

Maybe you can't relate to Karl. Maybe you've always been the kind of person who tried to get away with as much as you could. You've known that there was a set of rules in life, but it was made for others, not you. And you've never seen how your self-centeredness has caused so much trouble. You prefer to eat the frosting on the cake, before the cake; take the pleasure first, and try to block out the pain. Or maybe you have made a habit out of living next to the line.

M. Scott Peck, in his best-seller *The Road Less Travelled*, talks about the importance of learning to delay gratification. "Delaying gratification is a process of scheduling the pain and pleasure of life in such a way as to enhance the pleasure by meeting and experiencing the pain first and getting it over with. It is the only decent way to live" (Simon and Schuster, p. 19).

Moral Choices

Each and every day we are asked to make choices. Many of those choices are not critical. But each and every choice fits into a certain way that we view the world. Either those behaviors fit in with our values, or they violate our values. For most of us, we tend to not think about how our choices reinforce our standards. We have become numb to our internal values. Let's take a moment and think about some of the choices we have made recently.

● What are some of the right choices you have made recently which fit in with your moral values? _____

_____

_____

_____

● Share a recent experience where you chose to delay gratification: _____

_____

_____

_____

● How does making right choices feel? _____

_____

_____

● How do those right choices affect those around you? _____

_____

_____

The point here is not to beat ourselves up for our moral failures. Heaven knows, and God does too, that we cannot help but be the kinds of people we are. But we can become more aware of how we violate our own standards and how destructive that is to us in the long run. When we truly care for ourselves and love ourselves, we won't want to violate our own or others' boundaries. We realize that limits are there for our own protection.

"Children need discipline to feel secure; so do adults. Discipline means understanding that there are logical consequences to our behavior. Discipline means taking responsibility for our behavior and the consequences. Discipline means learning to wait for what we want. Discipline means being willing to work for and toward what we want" (_The Language of Letting Go,_ Melody Beattie, Harper/Hazelden, p. 327).

The Image of God

"So God created man in His own image, in the image of God He created him; male and female He created them" (Genesis 1:27). There are hundreds of volumes in theological libraries that deal with the image of God in man. There is no way that we could explain all the meaning in these and other verses that deal with man in the image of God. On an everyday level we are more aware of how we are NOT like God than how we are like God. Our limitations are staggering when compared to God's infinite qualities.

However, there are some practical insights we can gain if we look at one way in which we are like God. Like God, we have the ability to choose. Unlike God, we have the ability to choose poorly. Our first parents, Adam and Eve, illustrate this well. God gave them a choice concerning the Tree of the Knowledge of Good and Evil. God wanted them to know the difference between good and evil by choosing and experiencing good. Instead they came to know the difference between good and evil by choosing and experiencing evil. And that has become the experience of us all.

Though the image of God in man was altered by the Fall, it was not lost. Man still has the ability to choose the right. But our tendency or bent is toward evil. We are born that way (Ephesians 2) and our flesh is still that way (Romans 7). One of the great things about the Gospel is that we gained more in Christ than we lost in Adam. As we are conformed to the image of Christ, we have His righteousness, something Adam never had.

Moral Failure

Unfortunately, all of us reading and participating in this workbook have made errors in the paths we have chosen. We know of leaders who seemingly have always chosen the right path, but that doesn't fit us. It is very tempting to believe that we are alone in our struggle with right and wrong, and that we alone have chosen incorrectly. This is a myth perpetuated by all who try to look good. And let's face it—we *all* want to look good. This seems to be a trait built into human nature. As we strive to pretend that we don't make mistakes, we further isolate ourselves and increase our guilt and shame for the mistakes that we know are under the surface. What relief there is in coming out with our struggles. It is very freeing to acknowledge that we are imperfect and have natural weaknesses. "For all have sinned and come short of the glory of God" (Romans 3:23).

But what if we have made some really big mistakes? Perhaps you struggle with pornography, or you are involved in an affair, or your wife has left you because of your temper. Perhaps you have been dishonest in business, or you have lied to protect your reputation, or you have harmed others physically. The list could go on and on. Is there a crime or sin that we could mention that would put you in an entirely different category and make you completely unworthy as a person? We suspect you will answer yes to that question. And the interesting thing is that most of us feel that way deep within ourselves. There is a core part of us that feels bad; not just that we have done something wrong and made mistakes, but subsequently, that we are bad. That we do not measure up to others. They are somehow better than we are. This is the nature of shame and explains the importance of coming out of hiding and sharing our burdens one with another. "Carry each other's burdens, and in this way you will fulfill the law of Christ" (Galatians 6:2).

It is a freeing experience to open up and share our struggles with each other. This happened while we conducted a class for couples on the topic of biblical marriage. The first lesson was the "Perfect Marriage"—Adam and Eve. We emphasized the "ideal relationship," which made us all uncomfortable. The second lesson was "What Happened to That Perfect Marriage?" We dealt with the introduction of sin and its devastating consequences on that first marriage. Then we made this statement: "Since Adam and Eve, there are no more perfect marriages. We all have hang-ups. I came into my marriage with hang-ups, my wife came with her hang-ups and so did you." You could see a visible sigh of relief. Whew, it was OK to not have a perfect marriage. The rest of the time we dealt with handling our hang-ups, hang-ups with leadership, submission, children, finances, sex, etc. We mention this to say that once it was OK to have a hang-up, our discussions became open and constructive; we weren't trying to fake it but were addressing our failures openly and forthrightly.

In discussing the idea that we struggle with the concepts of success and failure, Erwin Lutzer, in his helpful book *Failure: The Back Door to Success,* says:

> There is a mixture of both in us all. In fact, it is only as we understand failure and accept it that we discover the secret of success. Often the doorway to success is entered through the hallway of failure. Our sins are a forcible reminder of our need for God's grace; our weaknesses make us appreciate God's strength. An understanding of our frailty is the basis for a dynamic relationship with God (Moody Press, 1975, p. 30).

Self-Exploration

● How have you tried to portray a perfect family (marriage or job) to others?

_____

_____

● How important to you is it to always be "right"? Explain:_____

_____

_____

_____

- List two areas of your life where you have struggled and failed: _____

_____

_____

- How do you feel about these mistakes? _____

_____

_____

- Who have you told about your moral failures? Do you need to go back over Step Five? _____

_____

_____

- Illustrate the statement "Failure is the back door to success" from personal experience: _____

_____

_____

- How does admitting our failures affect how we see others who fail? _____

_____

_____

- How do you feel about the likelihood that you will make mistakes in the future?

_____

_____

Step Seven Application

We humbly asked Him to remove our shortcomings.

"If we confess our sins He is faithful and just to forgive us our sins and purify us from all unrighteousness" (1 John 1:9).

In Step Six we made the conscious choice to let God remove our defects of character. We are now slowly realizing that all of our struggles to change will inevitably end in failure. This thing is bigger than we are. What we can do is to ready ourselves for the change process, and have patience. That which took a lifetime to create will not disappear overnight.

The second word in this step, *humbly,* has thrown a lot of people off course. This word implies that we acknowledge that we need help. We cannot do it alone. This part of the program keeps coming back to us. We are so used to doing things on our own. It is not easy to ask God or others for help. In fact, for many, the willingness to reach out for help is a good sign that we recognize our limitations. Be prepared that this action may be a very difficult part of this and other steps. Will you reach out and ask for help?

When we are truly ready to change, it will be amazing to find how much help is available. God is ready to help us and may use others—such as pastors, friends, and professionals—to help us find our way. Reaching out to others and telling them that our life isn't working can be a terrifying experience. Yet it must be done. It is part of the healing process.

Some of you may be frightened of change. We all know the feelings and attitudes of wanting to change, yet fear what we will become if we do change. I (Dave) have often thought of change as a bridge. We cross over the bridge from one manner of being to another, and that bridge can be frightening. Fortunately, we take with us across the bridge many strengths and traits that have been helpful to us. And we do not travel alone—God is there walking with us.

There is another thought that can be helpful for your journey: You cannot imagine how wonderful things are on the other side. Staying stuck is not a place of growth for you. Yes, it is a place of safety, in a way. But taking the bridge of growth is much more rewarding. You will like it on the other side!

For most of us, we have two very distinct fears:

1. That we will not really change. We will be that exception to the program, forever stuck with all the old baggage we desperately want to leave on this side of the bridge.

2. That we will change and not like the new person we are becoming.

Not to worry! If you are sincere in your desire to change, change will happen. And furthermore, you are the one to decide what traits you want to take with you. Have fun with the process of creating and exploring new parts of you that have been buried for a long, long time.

● List again the two or three shortcomings which you would like God to remove:

_____

_____

● What will be the benefit to yourself and others when God removes these shortcomings? _____

_____

_____

_____

● In what areas have you already seen growth? _____

_____

_____

"Do not be anxious about anything, but in everything, by prayer and petition, with thanksgiving, present your requests to God" (Philippians 4:6).

● Can you see how, through prayer and meditation, you are establishing a relationship with God which is healing you?_____

_____

_____

● How do you feel about this? _____

_____

_____

Professional Experience

It seems to me (Dave) that knowing who we are, what our values are, and setting out to align our lives around them are critical issues. Yet just as important as knowing our values and seeking to live by them, is understanding that we will have setbacks and failures. I believe there are several ways we can harm ourselves when it comes to our values and ethics. The first is to not be clear with ourselves as to what is important to us: what we value. The second is to not acknowledge when we have failed to live up to our standards. The third is to beat ourselves up emotionally when we deviate from our values in some way.

Life is a series of setting goals and missing them. Rarely, I believe, do we simply set a goal, hit it, and then move on to another. Oh, I wish it were that simple, but I don't believe that it is. We aim for a target with the best of intentions and then proceed to over- or undershoot the target. That "miss" helps us determine what our next shot should be. As the program says, "Progress, not perfection."

It is helpful for all of us to sit down at various times and decide what is important to us. What are my standards? What is important to me? How have I arrived at my ethical standards? How have I treated myself when I "miss the mark"? Did it help me clarify my values in some way?

Recovery Affirmations

There is a power greater than yourself ready to help you change. If you are ready and willing, He will guide you into those areas needing change today.

This week, on a daily basis, affirm that:

- God is willing and able to remove my character flaws;

- He will empower me to change, a little at a time;

- There is a new me waiting to be developed;

- The change process will be an exciting and rewarding journey.

Seventh Step Prayer

My Creator,

I am now willing that you should have all of me, good and bad. I pray that you now remove from me every single defect of character which stands in the way of my usefulness to you and my fellows. Grant me the strength, as I go out from here, to do your bidding.

Amen.

From *The Big Book of Alcoholics Anonymous* (Alcoholics Anonymous World Services, Inc., New York, N.Y., p. 76).

Eight

Men and Feelings

Jackie was extremely frustrated! This was the last straw. She told Mac that either they go to see a marriage counselor this week, or she would move out until they did. He was baffled. If anything, Mac considered himself to be too good of a listener. He rarely interrupted—he didn't dare—and he could repeat back to her everything she said.

"But you don't let me know that you are listening to me," she complained. "You don't really talk back to me! I do most of the talking. You don't ask me how my day has gone, or what I am worrying about. You don't share your feelings with me. It always feels like we are in two separate worlds."

To this Mac threw up his arms and stormed out of the room. There was no sense arguing with her, he decided. Her mind was made up, and maybe she would forget about her threat in a day or two. Mac simply could not understand where Jackie was coming from. A week later she was gone.

John Powell, in his magnificent little book *Why Am I Afraid to Tell You Who I Am?* (Tabor Publications, 1969), says that there are five levels of communicating. Try to honestly assess where you spend most of your time.

1. *Cliché Conversation.* Here we keep the topic light, talking about the weather and so on.

2. *Reporting the Facts.* On this level we talk about facts, such as the news, but still reveal little about ourselves.

3. *Giving Judgments.* Here we begin to reveal a little about ourselves. We share our attitudes and judgments about certain events.

4. *Reporting Feelings.* Now we are really sharing ourselves. At this level we are sharing something very personal, our feelings.

5. *Gut Level Communication.* At this "deepest" level we share all about ourselves, and

the result is honest communication. At this level we share our thoughts, attitudes, judgments, and, of course, our feelings.

Men are at a distinct disadvantage when it comes to honest, gut-level communication. We have been trained, in our culture, to value thinking and action, as opposed to feelings. We are to be problem solvers, men who "seize the day" and take control of every situation. It is quite foreign to consider the idea of reflection, contemplation, solitude, and active listening. Incidentally, by active listening, we mean taking delight in simply being there with the person and showing him, verbally and nonverbally, that we are trying to understand everything he is saying.

Most men need to take a big step before they are truly equipped to "be there" with another person. Before we can self-forget, which is necessary in order to be able to tune in to others, we must get to know ourselves. This requires time spent alone, understanding how we have arrived at where we are, where we are going, and how we intend to get there. Again, Sam Keen says that "the unavailable man is encumbered with himself. His preoccupation may take the form of an obsession with money, power, reputation, health, psychoanalysis, or even his spiritual journey. . . . For the unavailable man, life is a bank account and he always calculates how he spends and gives of himself" (*Fire in the Belly,* p. 157).

When we get in touch with ourselves and embark on the inner journey, a wonderful thing happens. We then become available to others. When we give up the notion that we are self-contained and understand that we really need others, we want to be near others and share in their exploration of the world. M. Scott Peck has defined *love* as "the will to extend one's self for the purpose of nurturing one's own or another's spiritual growth" (*The Road Less Travelled,* p. 1).

Mac was afraid that Jackie's criticisms might be right. At times he felt out of touch with even himself. He always felt alone in his world. Though he could say that he had a few buddies with whom he went hunting, and he was friendly with several of the guys at work, he knew that he struggled with letting people really know him and in taking the time to get to know others. What was the risk of tuning in to his feelings? Why did he create elaborate schemes (defenses) in order to avoid experiencing painful emotion?

Unfortunately, this is the lifestyle many of us are living. Instead of using our feelings as guideposts, beacons if you will, we fear them and want to avoid pain at any cost. Perhaps this is the result of rational, Western culture. Consider such common expressions as "Look on the bright side" and "To every cloud there is a silver lining." This counsel is not all wrong, but somewhat misguided. What is needed is a clarity about our inner feelings, held up to the light of prayerful thoughtfulness, to help us determine what is missing in our lives. "Feelings, then, are the fine tunings directing the ways in which we will meet and manipulate our environment" (*Feelings,* Willard Gaylin, Ballantine, 1979, p. 7).

Self-Exploration

Please review this limited list of feelings, noting those with which you are most comfortable and those you avoid.

Sadness	Joy	Anger	Discouragement
Fear	Remorse	Delight	Anxiety
Apprehension	Excitement	Humility	Jealousy
Happiness	Wariness	Distrust	Cautiousness
Timidity	Shyness	Tiredness	Comfort
Envy	Silliness	Loneliness	Bitterness

● Which of these feelings do you find yourself able to express? _____

_____

_____

● Which of these feelings do you find yourself avoiding? Why? _____

_____

_____

● Which of these feelings were most often expressed in your family of origin?

_____

_____

● Were any of these feelings avoided or punished in your family of origin? If so, explain: _____

_____

_____

_____

● How has accepting your feelings recently been helpful to you?_____

_____

_____

_____

Real Manhood

Contrary to popular opinion, real manhood does not consist in being tough and macho. Insensitivity has no place in the life of the secure man. The secure man does not flaunt his accomplishments, and accepts the fact that he may be quite average in many areas of his life. Yet if he is listening carefully to God, he will be exploring innate, natural passions within him that are waiting to be developed.

Tom Eisenman, in his book *Temptations Men Face*, notes that Christian men are free to have the following common behaviors:
1. The Christian man is free to be a servant leader;
2. The Christian man is free to be lighthearted;
3. The Christian man is free to interact with others;
4. The Christian man is free to be tender;
5. The Christian man is free to stand for righteousness;
6. The Christian man is free to be concerned for the world around him (InterVarsity Press, 1990, pp. 43-44).

Step Eight Application

We made a list of all persons we had harmed and became willing to make amends to them all.

"Do to others as you would have them do to you" (Luke 6:31).

Here is where the rubber meets the road, so to speak. This is very difficult work. It is usually easier to remember wrongs done to us, as opposed to wrongs we have done to others. But the Eighth Step asks us to list those we have harmed *and* to whom we are willing to make amends. Sometimes we are clear about whom we have harmed, but are not yet ready to let go of our feelings about them.

The task here is not to lay a huge guilt trip about our past behavior. Quite the opposite. We want to "clean the slate" so we can move on with our lives. It will be important that we do this work with lots of support and guard against the tendency to punish ourselves for past behavior.

We have repeatedly said in this workbook that much of the healing possible for us comes from getting honest with ourselves. We cannot truly forgive ourselves if we haven't first been honest with ourselves. It is so natural to want to take shortcuts in this process. We call this easy forgiveness, because true in-depth healing has not taken place.

The Scriptures teach us that forgiveness is a two-way street. "Forgive us our trespasses as we forgive those who trespass against us...." This is quite a sobering thought, that forgiveness runs both ways. Is it possible that our ability to be forgiven hinges to a certain extent on how we forgive others?

What a freeing step this is! Most of us are carrying around baggage from past relationships and don't see how this negatively impacts our lives now. We would remind those who glibly say, "Out of sight, out of mind," that the mind forgets nothing, especially those conflicts that we are hanging onto from our past. And as we review troublesome areas, we learn the lessons that we are supposed to learn. Otherwise, we are doomed to repeat mistakes.

For some, working this step may not only be frightening, but seem selfish. The task is to focus on ourselves, looking at what we have done to harm others. In almost all problematic relationships, all parties share some of the responsibility for things going sour. While it is tempting to play the "blame game," this is not helpful to anyone. Look at your part in the problems. How have you contributed to the difficulties that took place?

Amends List Guidelines

The following are a few ideas about how to approach the Amends List, taken from the book, *The Twelve Steps for Christians* (Recovery Publications, 1988). The authors suggest that there are three main categories in which we may have caused harm, and for which we must be willing to make amends.

Material Wrongs: Actions which affected a person in a material way, such as:
- Borrowing or spending extravagance; stinginess; spending in an attempt to buy friendship or love; withholding money in order to gratify yourself.
- Entering into agreements that are legally enforceable, then refusing to abide by the terms or simply cheating.
- Injuring or damaging persons or property as a result of our actions.

Moral Wrongs: Inappropriate behavior in moral or ethical actions and conduct, including questions of rightness, fairness, or equity. The principal issue is involving others in our wrongdoing:

- Setting a bad example for children, friends, or anyone who looks to us for guidance.
- Being preoccupied with selfish pursuits and totally unaware of the needs of others.
- Inflicting moral harm (e.g., sexual infidelity, broken promises, verbal abuse, lack of trust, lying).

Spiritual Wrongs: "Acts of omission" as a result of neglecting our obligations to God, to ourselves, to family and to community.
- Making no effort to fulfill our obligations and showing no gratitude toward others who have helped us.
- Avoiding self development (e.g., health, education, recreation, creativity).
- Being inattentive to others in our lives by showing a lack of encouragement to them (p. 82).

In making an Amends List, try to be as specific as possible, being clear about the effect of your behavior on others and how it impacted you as well. What exactly did you do that created harm? What needs to be done to make amends?

"Why do you look at the speck of sawdust in your brother's eye and pay no attention to the plank in your own eye? How can you say to your brother, 'Let me take the speck out of your eye' when all the time there is a plank in your own eye? You hypocrite, first take the plank out of your own eye, and then you will see clearly to remove the speck from your brother's eye" (Matthew 7:3-5).

Jesus' words give us the order and proper strategy for making amends with our brothers. Here Christ reveals that the greatest hindrance to making amends is feeling that the bigger fault lies with my brother. Yes, I was wrong, but he was mostly wrong. It is a matter of perspective. A speck of sawdust in another's eye is a beam in one's own eye. I may think that I am only 10 percent wrong, but in his eye, I am 90 percent wrong. Therefore, the first step is to remove my fault; then I will be able to see clearly.

- So let's begin by listing all the people who we have wronged. Next to their names list the nature of the harm you have done (Material, Moral, Spiritual) and how you can make amends. A review of Step Four will help you to remember who should be on your list. Next, make a similar list for those who have harmed you. For now, focus only on the names and offenses to be put on your lists. We will deal with the actual "how to's" of it later.

Names of persons I have harmed	The nature of the injury	The nature of amends	Date amends were made
1_____	_____	_____	_____

2 _____ _____ _____ _____

3 _____ _____ _____ _____

4 _____ _____ _____ _____

5 _____ _____ _____ _____

6 _____ _____ _____ _____

7 _____ _____ _____ _____

8 _____ _____ _____ _____

9 _____ _____ _____ _____

10 _____ _____ _____ _____

● What is it that makes asking forgiveness so hard to do? _____

_____

_____

● Why would someone not want to forgive you? _____

_____

_____

● God is interested in our making amends to those we have harmed. Even though we don't make animal offerings (Christ offered Himself once for all), there are principles of restitution that we would do well to follow. Read Leviticus 6:1-7 and answer the following questions:

1. When we harm a brother, whom have we really been unfaithful to? _____

_____

2. List the types of offenses mentioned which need restitution: _____

_____

_____

3. What is the standard principle for making restitution? _____

_____

_____

Names of persons who have harmed me	The nature of the injury	Date forgiveness was initiated
1_____	_____	_____
2_____	_____	_____
3_____	_____	_____
4_____	_____	_____
5_____	_____	_____
6_____	_____	_____
7_____	_____	_____
8_____	_____	_____
9_____	_____	_____
10_____	_____	_____

• What is it that makes forgiving someone so hard to do? _____

_____

_____

• Why would someone refuse to forgive? _____

_____

_____

● As mentioned before, our expectation of being forgiven is based on our forgiveness of others. Read Matthew 18:21-35 and answer these questions:

1. How often am I expected to forgive my brother? _____

_____

2. Why did Jesus tell this story?_____

_____

_____

3. Why did the king call his servant a wicked servant?_____

_____

_____

4. What was the application that Jesus made of this story?_____

_____

_____

Professional Experience

For most men, it can be a very difficult task to take the inward journey, reflecting on how we have ignored our feelings. It seems so impractical. There are problems to be solved, jobs to be done, achievements to be made. To spend time looking within seems so fruitless.

But feelings *must* be worked through. This all takes time and energy to find our emotional center where we can process things that have been done to us or by us. Most men find it hard to give themselves permission to take the time and place necessary to process feelings. There are rarely instant answers. It is very tempting to pretend that past events have no effect now over our lives. We call this denial.

We have found that not only do men struggle with allowing the painful feelings to surface, but they also squelch positive feelings which occur. Believe it or not, many men are afraid of feeling too good. Happiness, silliness, and joy were not allowed in their family of origin. Once the lid begins to loosen on the painful feelings, there will be a freeing of the positive ones as well.

Recovery Affirmations

Congratulations! You are working through the Twelve Steps, showing that you are serious about changing. Working these transformational steps and relying on God will change you, slowly but surely.

This next week, on a daily basis, affirm that:

- I am willing to make amends to the persons I have harmed;

- God will guide me in this process;

- I am growing and changing into a new creation;

- I will be more self-respecting for doing this work.

Eighth Step Prayer

Dear Lord,

Please encourage me, Lord, to do the work that You are leading me to do.
Help me to have courage as I move forward.
Remind me that I don't have to change to have Your love.
You love me just the way I am.
And give me strength to affirm all of my feelings,
even the ones I may want to ignore.

Amen.

Nine
Men and Money

As Jack zapped the remote control, searching for something of interest to watch on TV, he paused to watch the commercial for the popular fragrance "Virility." It showed a muscular young man with an adoring, bikini-clad woman on the deck of an expensive sailboat, the wind blowing through their hair. They were smiling affectionately at each other as the sailboat cut through the water at a 30-degree angle. Their closeness was obviously due to the fragrance he wore—at least that's what the announcer insisted.

Jack wondered what it would be like to live like that, to have his own boat, a gorgeous woman, and enough money to do whatever he wanted. Something stirred inside; he had to admit that the image appealed to him. He knew he was being bombarded with media "hype" to influence him in a direction he probably shouldn't go. But that sailboat and woman looked awfully good. What would it take?

The underlying message: Money is power, power to do and to have what you want! Jack knows that he is not the man in the commercial. He doesn't have the looks, he doesn't have the physique, he doesn't have the boat, he doesn't have a girlfriend, and he doesn't have the money. Jack falls short. Comparisons always do that to us, you know. Madison Avenue taps into our feelings of inferiority, in the hopes that we will go out and buy that fragrance, so that we will have what the man in the commercial has. Think about it. If Jack buys "Virility," will the rest follow? Then why are so many men buying "Virility"?

The local bookstore is another place where Jack gets bombarded with the same message. There are many "get rich quick" books with enticing titles like *Think and Grow Rich, Wealth Without Risk,* and *Creating Wealth.* The authors say financial success is possible for anyone willing to try. Why shouldn't Jack go after it?

Jacques Ellul, in his book, *Money and Power,* says, "Money has become the criterion for judging man and his activity. One by one, the state, the legal system, art and the churches have submitted to the power of money" (InterVarsity Press, p. 20). There is a subordination of *being* to *having.* Sadly, in our society, the worth of the man is literally determined by his monetary worth. Or to put it another way, a man's self-worth is measured by his net worth.

But just as quickly as we aspire to have all the goodies that we see in the media and all around us, at some level we also know that everything is not as it seems. The man on the sailboat may actually not be as happy as he looks. The corporate executive who works sixteen-hour days may have the externals of success, but is he really happy? We can see the glitz and glamour of Hollywood, but we also know of the divorces and addictions that go with the territory.

It is a myth that "money is the key to happiness." Money holds a lot of promises, but fulfills very few.

A Parable

In Luke 12:16-21 a parable is told of a rich man with a problem. His hard work had yielded an abundance of crops which he had no place to store. So he decided to build bigger storehouses to house the surplus. Then, as the story goes, he thought that he would take life easy. At that point: "God said to him, 'You fool! This very night your life will be demanded from you. Then who will get what you have prepared for yourself?' This is how it will be with anyone who stores up things for himself but is not rich toward God."

The rich man in Jesus' story died before he could begin to use what was stored up in his big barns. The moral is that if we are storing up goods only to enrich ourselves it will be of no value when we have to face God. Only spiritual richness will matter then. Therefore, we must be concerned about our spiritual richness, our richness toward God—*now*.

Money: A Healthy Perspective

Remember, money is not the root of all evil, but rather the love of it (1 Timothy 6:10). Money serves a valuable function when it is used to support ourselves and our families, to build hospitals, to send relief to starving people, to send medical workers into remote areas, and to support missionaries translating the Bible into a formerly unwritten language. No, money is neither good nor bad in and of itself. It is our attitude toward money and how we handle money that gives it the power for good or the power for evil.

We are all given opportunities to make money, and we must decide how much we need to live on and when we simply have enough. Ultimately, we recognize that all the resources available to us belong to God. They have been entrusted to us temporarily, but they still belong to Him. It is very tempting to believe otherwise. "The earth is the Lord's, and everything in it, the world, and all who live in it" (Psalm 24:1).

Jacques Ellul notes, and we would agree, that wealth usually leads to some kind of downfall. He states that wealth is temptation "because it urges us to put confidence in money rather than in God" (p. 47). When we have any measure of wealth, we start to believe in ourselves and in our own resources. Not only do we put our trust in ourselves, but we go a step further. We deny God. "Sheltered by our riches, we quickly mistake ourselves for God" (p. 48). We, being human, and disposed toward addictions, don't know how not to become obsessed with something. We have an incredible ability to take this object, money, and make it our god, in many cases destroying our quality of life.

In order to combat the teachings we get from the media and society, we need to have another set of standards to which we can adhere. We suggest that the most important thing for any of us to do concerning money is to know what the Scriptures teach on the topic. Jesus talked a great deal about money. Most of what He had to say was aimed at the importance of not living for the pursuit of money. To live for money and what we can obtain with it is a very shallow existence. Christ repeatedly stated that it was in losing that we gain. He teaches us that we need to lay our lives down for others, and this includes our money.

An increasing number of men are taking these words of Jesus seriously: "A man's life does not consist in the abundance of his possessions" (Luke 12:15). These men are developing another set of monetary standards to live by, and they are achieving interesting results. Instead of moving frantically through life, looking for the next get-rich-quick scheme, they are slowing down and simplifying their lives. They have decided that more material things usually mean more headaches. Instead of accumulating more and more, they are giving more away. They are vowing, and succeeding at, not letting money control their moods and mindset. Ron Blue notes that the mark that distinguishes the Christian from the world "is the absence of anxiety over the prospect of losing some possession. The Christians' treasure is stored in heaven, not on this earth. Really believing this frees us to give generously to God's purpose and His people" (*Charisma*, January 1992, p. 23).

While advertising strives to tell us that we need more and more to be happy, we can decide to be happy with what we have. There is a proverb that says, "Happiness is not having what you want, but wanting what you have." This is so true and is an important principle for our recovery. Another aspect of this truth is enjoying the possessions of another without desiring to possess them for ourselves.

An antidote for hoarding, which is commonplace among those pushing to get to the top, is sharing. This is another sign of authentic Christianity, sharing with those who are less fortunate. Wealth is not meant to be something which we use to lavish more and more luxuries upon ourselves. We might be surprised to see our attitude toward money change as we become generous with others. Let go of money and concentrate on living!

Self-Exploration

● How does money tempt you? _____

_____

_____

● What are some things worth going into debt for? _____

_____

_____

● Does making money help fill an empty place within you? Explain: _____

_____

_____

● Do you admire wealthy people? Who? Why? _____

_____

_____

_____

● Are you tempted to see yourself as "who you are is what you have"? _____

_____

_____

● In what ways have you developed a lifestyle driven by money? _____

_____

_____

● How do you feel about the idea of developing a simpler lifestyle? _____

_____

_____

_____

● What are the barriers to a simpler lifestyle? _____

_____

_____

_____

Step Nine Application

We made direct amends to such people wherever possible, except when to do so would injure them or others.

"Therefore, if you are offering your gift at the altar and there remember that your brother has something against you, leave your gift there in front of the altar. First, go and be reconciled to your brother, then come and offer your gift" (Matthew 5:23-24).

At this point in your Twelve Step work, you have made lists (those you've harmed, those who've harmed you) and are prepared to take the next step in making amends to people. Your awareness has been heightened by the time you have taken to prepare the lists. It can be frightening to see all the areas of our lives that we have denied. How were we able to keep all of this pain outside of our awareness? These are the feelings that have created fuel for the struggling relationships we have had, and bad moods that we could never explain. But we are now better prepared to take a closer look.

Have you made your list of people who have harmed you? Are you clear about the effect they have had on your life? Rather than just focusing on how "bad" they were, and getting into the victim role, think about what impact they had on you. Why did their behavior have such an impact on you? Could it be that their behavior was an echo of some situation in your past that has not been resolved?

There is some truth to the idea that people cannot make you feel any particular way. Something unique to your makeup has a large impact on why you respond the way you do. If you can understand and accept this, it will go a long way toward helping you to let go of resentment toward others for what they have done to you.

It will be important not to rush forgiveness. When you are ready to forgive, it will happen. Many seem to think that forgiveness is a once-for-all event. It can more accurately be described as a process, often happening a little at a time. Don't be alarmed if painful feelings remain with you for some time. Again, look at what the feelings may be triggering within you.

In most cases, the people who have harmed you have also been harmed by you. It is easy to see others' part in the problem but not so easy to see our part. Critically look at those relationships where tension exists, and see if you have contributed to the problems in any way.

Step Nine says that we "made amends to such people wherever possible." It will not always be possible to go back and make amends. Attitude and willingness to make amends are the keys here. As you pray about who needs an amend, you may be surprised at who comes into your mind. When it is impossible to make an amend to the person injured, you may want to do some special kindness to an unrelated person as a gesture of your good will. The important issue is that you reflect to someone, somewhere, that you have changed and recognize the error of your ways.

Step Nine goes on to say, "Except when to do so would injure them or others." It is never easy to decide whether to be totally truthful to people or to withhold some information in order to protect them. Much of the time we may really be trying to protect ourselves and may use this as a way to avoid personal pain. It may be best to seek counsel if you are in doubt about how direct to be with these people in your life.

Finally, we should not forget to be willing to make amends to ourselves. In many cases, we have harmed ourselves as much, if not more, than others. List the ways that you have been harsh with yourself. In what ways have you been unloving toward yourself? How do you treat others more kindly than you treat yourself?

As you complete this step, use some of the following guidelines:

- Devote time to prayer regarding your amends;
- Treat yourself lovingly and kindly;
- Remember that we all make mistakes;
- Most will be thankful for your efforts.

A last word about financial amends is in order. Money has been a controlling influence in many of our lives. Either we have driven ourselves to obtain more of it, and been hoarders, or perhaps we have been at the other end of the scale. That is, we have decided not to take financial responsibilities seriously and have gotten ourselves into serious debt. Perhaps we have borrowed more money than we knew we could repay. We may have lived with an attitude of "Play now, pay later." Perhaps we have cheated others out of their fair share. The point here is that money is often an integral part of our amends. Take a special look at how money may be a part of your amends program.

Taking responsibility for our finances in a healthy way may cause us some discomfort in the short run. We may have to pay someone back to whom we owe money. Or we may decide to live a lifestyle well within our means, which will be uncomfortable. But growth will happen, and we will be on our way toward a peaceful existence.

● What is the easiest situation in which to make an amend? _____

_____

_____

_____

● What is the most difficult? _____

_____

_____

● What is it like to make amends to yourself? _____

_____

_____

_____

"Give and it will be given to you. A good measure, pressed down, shaken together and running over, will be poured into your lap. For with the measure you use, it will be measured to you" (Luke 6:38).

● What are your thoughts about this verse? _____

_____

_____

Professional Experience

In my (Dave's) private practice I see so many people who are driven by fear. While I used to believe that the emotion of shame was the biggest obstacle to peaceful living, I am wondering if fear ought to take its place at the top of the list.

I have seen that in the lives of so many, fear has caused them to grasp onto things anxiously, for fear that things can never be replaced. Fear seems to have driven many to compete with one another rather than to live in harmony and share resources. This, of course, leads to lives of isolation and emptiness.

When we live lives based on competition and who can accumulate the most, we breed distrust because we never know who will try to rob us of what we have. In this material-crazed world there are no friends, only foes. We may act friendly, but secret distrust lies just below the surface.

It is risky, but we can live differently. We can "let go" and believe that good things will come our way. We can believe that we can get along with much less. We can find joy and satisfaction in helping others who are less fortunate. We can find nourishment in being connected to others, in sharing the things with which we have been blessed.

Recovery Affirmations

Step Nine teaches us to make amends with our world and with ourselves. This is a step which truly brings us back in contact with those with whom we have been estranged. We will be free to reach out to others again and will be free to treat ourselves more compassionately as well.

As this step relates to finances and material things, which are important to all of us, affirm this week that:

- I have enough money to be happy;

- Loving money is not healthy for me;

- I want to share the resources I have been given;

- God is the owner of everything.

Ninth Step Prayer

Dear Lord,

Strengthen me, Lord, to do the work of reconciliation.
I thank You for Your gracious gift of forgiveness for my sin.
Help me to extend Your love to those who have hurt and offended me.
Lord, give me the courage to ask forgiveness of those who I have hurt and offended.

Free us all from grudges and roots of bitterness.
Might we put away all wrath, clamor, and evil speaking
and love one another with a pure heart fervently.

Amen.

Ten

Reconciliation

There was a time, not long ago, when what happened to the Karns family would not have happened. Some would say that those were the "good old days." Others would say that they were the "Stone Ages," and it was good that we left them behind.

You would have no trouble deciding how Kim, Kari, and Kelli—six, seven, and nine years old—would cast their vote. They could not even understand the phrase "irreconcilable differences." When their parents tried to explain why they would no longer be living together as a family, they became even more confused. For most of their short lifetimes, things had gone along fine. What had changed? Why were there now things that could not be fixed? They could not help but feel very angry, hurt, betrayed, and abandoned. From their simple perspectives it seemed that their parents were just being stubborn and unreasonable.

Laws have changed, divorce is easy to obtain, and the divorce rate has continued to climb. The causes are numerous, but the term on the legal petition for marital dissolution is "irreconcilable differences." What this means, in so many words, is that there are areas of disagreement which the couple refuses to resolve.

Doug Karns was raised by parents who resolved conflicts by yelling and throwing things. Terrified by his parents' arguments, Doug had purposed to avoid all conflicts. At school he would avoid the area on campus where the "bullies" hung out. As a young man he quit a job rather than confront the boss. Now he was leaving his family rather than trying to work things out. Things had built up to the point that he didn't want to stay married anymore. The pleas of his kids, parents, and friends to reconcile with his wife didn't stop him from leaving. Doug had no concept of reconciliation. He had never seen it modeled and didn't believe it could occur.

Before we go further, we should explain in more detail what "reconciliation" is. *Vine's Expository Dictionary of New Testament Words* defines *reconciliation* as "a change from enmity to friendship." It is "primarily an exchange. . .a change on the part of one party, induced by an action on the part of another" (pp. 261-262).

Theodore Isaac Rubin, in the preface to his book *Reconciliations,* describes it well by saying:

> Reconciling is a mending and integrating process. It involves bringing aspects of self, and of self and others, together into relative mutual harmony. This is the antithesis of one aspect giving way to the other or of one being sacrificed for the other. For reconciliation to take place, blind compulsivity, pride, inner tyranny, and self-glorification must be reduced, as insight, humility, and humanity are increased (Viking, 1980).

In other words, at times we need to honor the relationship above ourselves.

In the Bible the Apostle Paul says:

"Do nothing out of selfish ambition or vain conceit, but in humility consider others better than yourselves. Each of you should look not only to your own interests, but also to the interests of others" (Philippians 2:3-4).

"Do not think of yourself more highly than you ought, but rather think of yourself with sober judgment" (Romans 12:3).

Paul isn't saying to ignore our own self interests, but to value the interests of others more than our own. One danger is to think of ourselves too highly. But the other extreme is to deny our own best interest. The values of both parties must be considered.

Communication, repentance, and forgiveness are all necessary parts of the process of reconciliation. Without communication, we cannot present our point of view, nor can we understand another's point of view. And when a relationship is ruptured through wrongdoing, without repentance we cannot gain the closeness needed for the friendship to continue. Of course, repentance must then be responded to with forgiveness.

These three elements are seen in the passage, "If your brother sins, rebuke him, and if he repents, forgive him. If he sins against you seven times in a day, and seven times comes back to you and says, 'I repent,' forgive him" (Luke 17:3-4).

Communication is seen in the rebuke of the erring brother as well as in the approachability of the offended brother, so much so, that, if necessary, the errant brother can come back seven times to seek forgiveness. As we saw in Matthew 7:5, it is assumed that we have already taken the plank out of our own eye and that we are seeing clearly our brother's fault. The word *rebuke* in this passage means to value a relationship enough to explain to your friend how he has offended you. "Rebuke" sounds harsh, but there is no harshness in the concept. I value my friendship enough to risk its continuance by clearly showing my friend wherein he is wrong. I then give him the freedom to recognize his error and repent. Now, that takes real courage and skill in communication. At the time, he may not see it my way, so I leave the way open through the unlimited nature of my availability for him to come to me later to seek my forgiveness and be reconciled.

When a brother comes to us and repents, we forgive him. "Be kind and compassionate to one another, forgiving each other, just as in Christ God forgave you" (Ephesians 4:32).

If we have experienced the forgiveness of our sins by God in Christ, we have the resources necessary to forgive our brother. The offense of our sin to God is huge. Our sin is odious to a holy God. Only the death of Christ could pay the penalty for our wickedness. Our brother's offense to us is small and puny in comparison. Since we have experienced such a great forgiveness, how dare we not forgive our brother? That is the point of Jesus' parable in Matthew 18:23-35.

This parable is about a servant who was forgiven a great debt of $9.6 million (based on the value of a denarii being $16). This forgiven servant subsequently finds a fellow servant who owes him $16 and demands to be paid. This second servant can't pay and begs for more time. The forgiven servant refuses and throws him into prison. When the master finds out about it, he says to the first servant, " 'Shouldn't you have had mercy on your fellow servant just as I had on you?' In anger his master turned him over to the jailers to be tortured, until he should pay back all he owed" (Matthew 18:33-34).

We can see the justice of that. But what is scary is Jesus's commentary on the parable. He says, "This is how My Heavenly Father will treat each of you unless you forgive your brother from your heart" (Matthew 18:35). Another way of saying it may be, if you don't forgive your brother, it is a good indication that you know nothing of forgiveness from God. If we have entered into the immensity of our forgiveness from God, we will not hesitate to forgive our brother his minor offenses.

Reconciliation with God

Many men are not reconciled with one another, with their spouses, with themselves, and ultimately, they are estranged from God. In fact, it is their relationship with God which needs most immediate attention. Remember, the earlier steps have taught us that our lives have become unmanageable and that we have become willing to turn our lives over to the power of God.

Perhaps more important than any other theme in this workbook is the theme of "healing through relationship." And here, in our relationship to God, is the ultimate healing. But for us to relate directly with the Almighty God, there had to be reconciliation—a reestablishing of relationship. Remember that we broke our relationship with God when we became terribly self-involved in the Garden of Eden. But God saw fit to reestablish a relationship with us by sending Christ to pay the penalty for our sinfulness. Paul writes:

> *Therefore, if anyone is in Christ, he is a new creation; the old has gone, the new has come! All this is from God, who reconciled us to Himself through Christ and gave us the ministry of reconciliation: that God was reconciling the world to Himself in Christ, not counting men's sins against them. And He has committed to us the message of reconciliation. . . . We implore you on Christ's behalf: Be reconciled to God. God made Him who had no sin to be sin for us, so that in Him we might become the righteousness of God (2 Corinthians 5:17-21).*

We have a ministry of reconciliation: man to God and man to man. When we are reconciled to God, we can share that healing message.

Communication

In order for reconciliation to take place, there must be serious communication. We have already made the case that many men are not skilled in this area. Men communicate much less than women do, often to the dismay of women. This seems to be in part a biological phenomenon, but it is also a sociological issue. Men in our culture are taught to keep their thoughts to themselves and to "play their cards close to their chest." Communication skills have not been taught or modeled for most men, and yet they are expected to be able to exercise them. When they haven't learned these skills, is it any wonder that they struggle to be able to share their thoughts and feelings? We trust that this workbook will help in this area.

Recovery involves coming out of hiding. There is only one way to do that—by sharing our story with others who care and will listen (Step Five). When we share our story, we are affirmed by our listeners, and we often get feedback. It is only through feedback that we learn if we are on the right track or not. In our isolated world, we are cut off from feedback that can signal us when we are heading too far in the wrong direction.

Anger

"I can't get him to express any of his personal feelings," said Judy, "except for anger." What Judy accuses her husband of seems to be, unfortunately, true of many men. They have been socialized not to show their tender or hurt feelings, but encouraged to show their "male toughness." The suppression of feelings is like trying to keep a beach ball under water. We can hold it down with great effort, but sooner or later it is going to spring free, spurt to the surface, and erupt with a big splash. Our multi-varied feelings of loneliness, fear, impotence, anxiety, lust, frustration, stress, and vulnerability all erupt into one outburst of anger. That is the one emotion we permit ourselves to express. That is, unless we are a Christians. Christians don't get angry, right? Wrong!

We all get angry, Christian or not, but our responsibility is to express our anger appropriately and constructively. Paul says, "In your anger do not sin: Do not let the sun go down while you are still angry" (Ephesians 4:26). So it is possible to be angry and not to sin. Problems in a relationship should not be left to simmer and steam overnight. We need to deal with them quickly. However, not many of us are doing that. The anger of men has caught the attention of popular writers. Have you noticed books on the subject with titles like *The Angry Man* and *Men Who Hate Women and the Women Who Love Them*?

The socializing of anger and toughness in men, however, has grown into a larger problem. Not only do men find it difficult to find the intimacy they need and the outlet for their hurts and frustrations, but the violence between men has grown to include violence between men and women. We have just come through a time which has introduced our culture to the phenomenon known, unfortunately, as the Battered Women's Syndrome. This syndrome, with its predictable stages, results in utter humiliation for both parties, as abuse becomes an attempted way to solve problems. Of course, it does not succeed, and the cycle simply repeats itself.

Men involved in battering relationships have been found to have some of the following difficulties:

- Difficulty in expressing feelings other than anger,
- Difficulty in interpersonal relationships with both sexes,
- Feelings of failure, inferiority and worthlessness,
- Poor communication and conflict resolution skills,
- Lacking in assertiveness and self-confidence,
- Lacking in self-discipline and organization,
- Tendency to abuse alcohol/drugs.

As you can see, the preceding list describes many men in today's culture. To curb violence toward women and toward each other, we must begin to change our attitudes about violence, and learn to express ourselves in healthier ways. We need to repent.

Speaking the Truth

One communication skill that could resolve some of the anger and violence problem is to "speak the truth in love" (Ephesians 4:15). If we love someone, we will tell him the truth. The truth may hurt the one who hears it, but the love will be felt and appreciated.

Sharon mentioned during a counseling session that Greg never snuggled with her in all their eleven years of marriage, and she didn't know why. The counselor asked Greg if that was true, to which Greg reluctantly nodded. The counselor then asked Greg why he didn't want to hold his wife close. Greg was noticeably uncomfortable and hesitant. The counselor encouraged him to tell the truth, and that Sharon really wanted to know.

Finally, Greg blurted out, "She has bad breath."

After an awkward moment the counselor asked, "Why haven't you told her before?"

"I didn't want to hurt her feelings," Greg replied.

Sharon's response was classic. "Yes, my feelings are hurt to know that I have bad breath. But it doesn't hurt as much as the last eleven years have hurt. I think that if you had really loved me, you would have told me long ago."

We need to love people enough to tell them the truth. If we tell them in a loving way, and tell them right away, hurt feelings won't fester into bitterness.

Listening

We are least schooled in the most important of the four principle means of communication (reading, writing, speaking, and listening). We learn to read and write in grammar school, in high school we have speech courses and drama classes, but where are we taught how to listen? Listening is the most important skill for understanding another person's point of view.

We want to be understood. It feels good to have been heard. We want others to see things from our perspective. Often this desire drives us so much that we don't really listen to what others are saying. While they are talking, we are thinking of the things we want to say next. Fortunately, men are learning that in order to get the closeness they desire, change must take place. They must learn to listen. The following are a few of the listening skills needed:

Paraphrasing: Sharing, in your own words, what you heard the person say.

"Let me rephrase what you have just said, so that I can be sure I have it right."
"In other words, what you are saying is. . . . Am I right?"
"Could I say it this way, and is that what you have in mind?"

Clarification: Asking the person if you are understanding what he is trying to say.

"What do you mean when you say. . . ?"
"Give me an illustration of what you are talking about."
"Do I understand you to mean. . . ?"

Questions: Asking leading questions to encourage sharing and to seek clarification.

"What do you see as the greatest obstacle we face?"
"How do you explain this?"
"What would cause a person to do that?"

Active Listening: Using gestures, eye contact, body posture, and verbal skills to show that you are actively involved in the conversation.

- Lean forward toward the person and look him in the eyes while talking.
- When the other person is angry, speak in a soft quiet tone.
- If you are too rushed now, set a time when you can talk.

Using these listening skills will improve communication. As we listen to others, we will see things, especially their hurts, from their point of view. It may even be that as we see their perspective, we will be deeply sorry for things we have done to hurt them and feel compelled to repent. Repentance and forgiveness result in reconciliation and lasting friendships.

Repentance

Genuine repentance is necessary for closeness in a restored relationship. When someone tells me he is sorry, but his attitude and verbal tone tell me that he doesn't really mean it, the distance in the relationship isn't removed. It is easy to see this when repentance is forced, as in the case with five-year-old Christopher when his mother ordered him: "Now, Christopher, tell your sister you are sorry, and do it now, or I will spank you." Christopher will probably comply in order to save his back side, but genuine repentance and reconciliation will not occur. However, when a person is sincerely sorry and my spirit senses it, I can readily forgive him. Closeness is restored. The relationship is reestablished.

What are the indications of sincere repentance? The Bible gives several tests so that we can know when repentance is sincere. For example, consider this passage:

"I am happy . . . because your sorrow led you to repentance. For you became sorrowful as God intended. . . . Godly sorrow brings repentance that leads to salvation and leaves no regret, but worldly sorrow brings death" (2 Corinthians 7:9-10).

Here Paul explains the difference between godly sorrow and worldly sorrow and goes on to list seven aspects of sincere repentance. Let's look at a few of these. Worldly sorrow leads to death, while godly sorrow leads to life. Worldly sorrow leaves regret, while godly sorry leaves no regret (v. 10). Genuine repentance is the result of being sorrowful as God intended (v. 9). Genuine repentance is first of all sorrow toward God, grief for offending Him and violating His moral standards. In contrast, incomplete or worldly repentance is sorrow for the consequences of our behavior.

Stan, an outside parts salesman for the local car dealership, was regularly getting speeding tickets because the more calls he made, the more money he made, and in his sales area the body shops were spread all over the state. Therefore, he put a "super snooper" radar detector on the dashboard of his car.

One day, Wendy, his sixteen-year-old daughter, went along with Stan on his rounds. They were traveling down the interstate when the super snooper sounded. Stan slowed the car down to 55 mph. Soon they passed a speed trap with several police cars. Stan nodded politely as they passed. Once out of range, he sped up to 75 mph again.

Now don't misunderstand; Stan is a well-respected member of the community. He is a deacon in the church and serves on the finance committee. He is not what you would call a "bad" person. However, what values did he teach on that business trip with Wendy? For one, it is only wrong if you get caught. Two, outward appearance is more important than inner reality. You see, as Stan passed those police officers, he "appeared" to be a law-abiding citizen, but both he and Wendy knew he was a law breaker.

This situation is particularly interesting because two years later Stan was outraged when he discovered that Wendy had secretly been taking birth control pills. When he confronted her, she silenced Stan by saying, "Dad, you have your super snooper and I have my super snooper. You are not going to get caught, and I am not going to get caught." What could he say? The discovery of his daughter's behavior is what prompted him to come for help.

Stan felt worldly sorrow over the speeding tickets, which led him to buy a super snooper in order to avoid the consequences. It wasn't "wrong" that he was speeding, it was only wrong when he got caught and had to pay a fine. His sorrow over Wendy's situation led him to see the deeper violation of God's principles. He inadvertently passed on his wrong value system. The evidence that his repentance was genuine was that he removed his super snooper and sought forgiveness from God. And that is the main indication of godly sorrow: It is God-focused.

Remember David's sin with Bathsheba? If not, read about it in 2 Samuel 11 and 12. David, upon repentance, records his confession of sin in Psalm 51. Speaking to God, he makes a remarkable statement when he says, "Against You, You only, have I sinned and done what is evil in Your sight" (v. 4). What? How can he say that? He lusted for Bathsheba. He committed adultery with her. He lied to her husband, got him drunk, and eventually had him killed. How in the world can he say, "Against You, You only, have I sinned and done what is evil in Your sight"?

Think about it. Who said that sex with your wife is wholesome and good, while sex with your neighbor's wife is wicked and wrong? Who said, "Thou shalt not commit adultery"? Bathsheba? Who said, "Thou shall not kill"? Uriah? No. GOD DID! When we sin, it is against God's law and against His commandments. Therefore, our repentance, if genuine, will be directed first to God. After that, it will be extended to others.

Nate and Joan have been married for twenty-seven years. Outwardly they have a good relationship. They get along well and enjoy the family. But Joan will tell you that even though they have been married for so long, they have never really been "close." She can even tell you why that is. The second year they were married, Nate went to summer camp with the National Guard. The guys went out on the town. Nate picked up a girl and spent the night with her. Several days after he returned, Joan was doing the laundry. Emptying Nate's fatigue pockets, she found a small note with a girl's name and phone number on it. Joan called the number and heard the girl's voice. Joan was devastated. When Nate got home, she confronted him. He laughed it off saying, "It was no big deal; boys will be boys." Joan was hysterical. She felt betrayed, humiliated, violated. After her emotional display, he said he was sorry, admitted it was wrong, and promised he wouldn't do it again. That was twenty-five years ago. Joan has no reason to suspect that Nate has ever been unfaithful since. Yet in her mind she reasons, "Nate has no idea how much he hurt me. If he did, I know he would never do it again. But because he doesn't see the seriousness of his actions, I am afraid that he might. I don't want to be vulnerable like that anymore, so I won't risk putting all my emotional eggs in his basket." So Joan keeps herself at arm's length emotionally because Nate never came to complete repentance.

Genuine repentance is required for closeness to be reestablished in a relationship that has been damaged by sin. This is true in our relationship with God and in our relationships with other people. Genuine repentance brings reconciliation and closeness.

Self-Exploration

● Which of the four listening skills (paraphrasing, clarification, questions, active listening) are you strongest in, and which one do you need to work on the most?

● Review the difficulties that some people have who are involved in a battering relationship. Do you see any of them in your life? If so, which ones? _____

_____

_____

● What things make you angry? _____

_____

_____

_____

● In what areas do you find it hard to "speak the truth in love?" _____

_____

_____

_____

● List those people from whom you currently feel separated: _____

_____

● What keeps you from reaching out to those people to seek reconciliation?

_____

_____

● How much of an issue is pride in our not reaching out to others? _____

_____

● List several activities where people seem to feel it is only wrong if you get caught:

_____

_____

● Are there any sins in your life (a mini Step Four) for which you have not come to complete repentance?_____

_____

_____

● Are there those who have sinned against you, but who have not expressed genuine repentance? Have you sought to lovingly rebuke them? Do you feel close to them?

_____

_____

_____

"We love because He first loved us. If anyone says 'I love God' yet hates his brother, he is a liar. For anyone who does not love his brother, whom he has seen, cannot love God, whom he has not seen" (1 John 4:19-21).

● What are your thoughts about these verses?_____

_____

_____

_____

Step Ten Application

We continued to take personal inventory and, when we were wrong, promptly admitted it.

"So, if you think you are standing firm, be careful that you don't fall!" (1 Corinthians 10:12)

There is no perfect recovery program. We must keep reminding ourselves of this important fact. We need to keep practicing what we have been learning and what we now know works. It works to take an inventory of our lives, repeatedly. That's one of the beautiful things about the Twelve Steps—they can be worked over and over again.

Step Ten gives us permission to be imperfect, which avoids the guilt trip we sometimes lay on ourselves. When I lose my temper and have unrealistic expectations of my kids, I can promptly admit being wrong. When I harbor a grudge and pout, when I try to manage others' lives, when I act smug and self-righteous—I can promptly admit being wrong.

That's the beauty of the Steps. I have permission to just be me, a piece of art that is still in the making. And, on a good day, I can allow you to be a piece of art in the making too. And if we happen to be together, it might just be a wonderful time!

The Tenth Step is also designed to keep our critical focus where it needs to be: on our lives, instead of on the lives of others. As you know, it is very tempting to get caught up in the "if only" game. You know, "If only she had done such and such, I'd be happy." Or, "If only I had such and such a thing, I'd be happy." This focus keeps us caught up on others, our future, or our past, so that today cannot truly be enjoyed.

The thought that others somehow control our happiness is an illusion that is bound to disappoint us. No, it does not require others to change for us to be happy. Our happiness is dependent on what *we* decide to do with our lives. It is very tempting to fall into:

- Focusing on others to the exclusion of ourselves,
- Trying to control the course of our relationships,
- Not being emotionally honest about our needs and feelings,
- Not being nurturing with ourselves,
- Letting fear control our lives,
- Being a martyr and depriving ourselves.

And when continuing to take a personal inventory, don't fall into the temptation of only highlighting the areas of difficulty. Remember to look at, and list, those areas that you manage effectively. What are the things you did well today? What relationships are going well for you?

- What are the things about you that you appreciate today? _____

_____

_____

_____

● How are you growing? How have you changed since starting the Twelve Step program? _____

_____

_____

_____

_____

● In what area(s) do you find yourself stuck? _____

_____

_____

Professional Experience

Wouldn't it be nice if progress would move in a straight path? We would just read the manual, take things step by step, and get on with life without a struggle. But, alas, that is not the way God made us. There are lessons to be learned, and this usually takes a great deal of time. Progress is usually more cyclical than linear. In other words, we try a new skill, make a little progress, slip back, lunge forward, fall back, and so on. We never get it perfect, though we do come close at times.

Accepting the imperfect recovery program is an important lesson. When we slip back into the doldrums, we need to look for underlying unfinished business. When we fear authority, we need to seek support. When we compare ourselves to others and feel inferior, we need to affirm our own strengths and seek God's help with our true identity.

Are you beginning to get a sense at times of the "peace that passes understanding"? The problems don't seem to disappear, but we feel God's presence with us through our struggles. Jesus said:

"I have told you these things, so that in Me you may have peace. In this world you will have trouble. But take heart! I have overcome the world" (John 16:33).

Recovery Affirmations

Now that we are more comfortable with ourselves, we find it easier to admit when we are wrong. We still may struggle with acknowledging new areas of work to be done, but even this comes more quickly than it used to. We now know that our self-esteem is not diminished when we admit difficulties, but rather it seems to be enhanced by our authenticity.

As we continue doing what works, we will focus this week on affirming:

- It's all right to have areas that still need work;

- I can admit mistakes more quickly;

- I will not hide from others;

- I will recognize that my offenses are basically against God;

- I seek reconciliation with God, myself, and others.

Step Ten Prayer

Dear God,

Keep showing me what I need to learn so that I can live a healthy, happy life. When wrong, help me to see its effect on You and others and to quickly admit it. When I do things well, help me to courageously affirm that within myself. Thank You for changing me, Father.

Amen.

Eleven

Meditation, Prayer, and God's Will

It has been said, "The proper study of mankind is man." More significantly, the proper study of the Christian is Christ. Charles Haddon Spurgeon once said:

> The highest science, the loftiest speculation, the mightiest philosophy, which can ever engage the attention of a child of God, is the name, the nature, the person, the work, the doings, and the existence of the great God whom he calls his Father.

> There is something exceedingly improving to the mind in a contemplation of the Divinity. It is a subject so vast, that all our thoughts are lost in its immensity; so deep, that our pride is drowned in its infinity. . . . No subject of contemplation will tend more to humble the mind, than thoughts of God. . . . But while the subject humbles the mind, it also expands it. . . . I know nothing which can so comfort the soul; so calm the swelling billows of sorrow and grief; so speak peace to the winds of trial, as a devout musing upon the subject of the Godhead.

This quote, taken from J.I. Packer's great book *Knowing God,* was delivered in a sermon at New Park Street Chapel on January 7, 1855, when Spurgeon was just twenty years old. It states eloquently the enormity of the activity of meditating on God. While we have already given some attention to the topic of prayer and meditation in Chapter 3, the topic is so critical that it deserves further exploration.

It is not our intent here to put a guilt trip on anyone. It is clear that because we men are "warrior" type individuals, trying to conquer our world, it is more difficult for us to be engaged in activities such as prayer and reflection. It seems very passive to us and not a fruitful investment of our time. Yet it is this preparation time, this time of musing on God, that is going to make us more effective and spiritually productive out there in the world.

An excellent book on keeping contact with God during a busy schedule is *Practicing the Presence of God* by Brother Lawrence. He was born Nicholas Herman in French Lorraine in 1611, and was converted to Christ at age eighteen. Eventually he became a Carmelite monk and took the name Brother Lawrence. He served that religious community working in the kitchen, and it was there amidst the pots and pans that he practiced the presence of God. He soon became known outside the community for his serene faith and his simple experience of God's presence. He received inquiries from all over France from people asking how to have a similar reality in their own daily experience with Christ. It was his letters of response, printed after his death in 1691, which became the book *Practicing the Presence of God.*

Meditation

The principle means for practicing the presence of God is meditation. In the Old Testament, *meditation* is the Hebrew word for chewing the cud. It has the idea of chewing on something over and over again in your mind, bringing it up again so you can chew on it some more. Unlike Eastern meditation practices which empty the mind, Christian meditation fills the mind with thoughts of good, God, and His Word. "Whatever is true, whatever is noble, whatever is right, whatever is pure, whatever is lovely, whatever is admirable—if anything is excellent or praiseworthy—think about such things" (Philippians 4:8).

God promises significant benefits for the man who doesn't just meditate, but meditates on the Word of God with the intent of doing what it says. "Do not let this Book of the Law depart from your mouth; meditate on it day and night, so that you may be careful to do everything written in it. Then you will be prosperous and successful" (Joshua 1:8).

Meditate on the Scriptures. Meditate on the truth that Christ lives within us. Consider the truth that sin no longer has a hold on us. Meditating on these truths can have a powerful impact on us. The psalmist experienced this when he reported: "Oh, how I love Your law! I meditate on it all day long. Your commands make me wiser than my enemies. . . . I have more insight than all my teachers, for I meditate on Your statutes. I have more understanding than the elders, for I obey Your precepts" (Psalm 119:97-100).

Meditating is a way of letting God speak to us through His Word. The other side of divine communication is our speaking to God through prayer.

Prayer

While it is important to set aside a daily time to converse with God, it is just as important to be involved in "prayerful living." The verse "Pray continually" (1 Thessalonians 5:17) does not mean to be on our knees constantly offering prayers to God. It means to always be in an attitude of prayer. This means keeping open contact with God at all times. Prayer should always be our first resort, not our last. When a distressing situation comes up, where do we turn? Often we exhaust our own resources before we turn to God in prayer. At the suggestion that we pray about it, someone is sure to say, "Has it come to that?" Such an attitude is not prayerful living.

Whenever we have a few moments, we can make contact with God through prayer and/or meditation. During our day we all have a few moments of idle time: a red light, a wait in the doctor's office, etc. These can be windows of opportunity for prayer and meditation.

Nehemiah is a good example of the balance between lengthy times of prayer and meditation and quick moments of prayer in a busy schedule. When Nehemiah's brother, Hanani, brought to the Persian Jews news of the terrible conditions in Jerusalem, Nehemiah spent considerable time before the Lord mourning, praying, and fasting. Later, when he resumed his duties he was asked by King Artaxerxes, "What is it you want?" Scripture records Nehemiah's response in Nehemiah 2:4: "Then I prayed to the God of heaven, and I answered the king. . . ." At a critical moment Nehemiah shot a quick prayer up to God before he gave the king his answer. We can do the same.

Our model for prayer is the prayer prayed by Christ Himself, now termed the Lord's Prayer. Read it through carefully and see what insights you come to in regards to your prayer life. Christ says:

> *This is how you should pray:*
> *"Our Father in heaven,*
> *hallowed be Your name,*
> *Your kingdom come,*
> *Your will be done,*
> *on earth as it is in heaven.*
> *Give us today our daily bread,*
> *Forgive us our debts,*
> *as we also have forgiven our debtors.*
> *And lead us not into temptation,*
> *but deliver us from the evil one"*
> *(Matthew 6:9-13).*

Following this pattern, our prayers should start off with adoration and recognition of God's high position. Next, our prayers will concern themselves with God's reputation and His program on the earth. After we have taken care of God's business, we turn to our needs—daily bread and forgiveness. Finally, our prayers should conclude with petitions of deliverance.

The Scriptures are very clear that we are to be in constant reliance upon God in order to succeed in this world. We are not to be dependent upon ourselves. And there is fruit and power available to us if we will pray and request it in Jesus' name. "You did not choose me, but I chose you to go and bear fruit—fruit that will last. Then the Father will give you whatever you ask in My name" (John 15:16).

Can you believe that the Father loves you and wants to give you good things? Doubting this fact, we believe, stops many from seeking God daily in prayer. Many believe God is "out there somewhere" but has little concern for our daily well-being. As you practice spending time with Him on a daily basis, you will begin to feel His presence and will look forward to spending time with Him. It takes faith to trust God completely, "and without faith it is impossible to please God, because anyone who comes to him must believe that He exists and that He rewards those who earnestly seek Him" (Hebrews 11:6).

As Christians, there are many resources that we do not use. When we are saved, we not only are reconciled to God, but we also are being transformed into the image of God in our lives. What does this mean? It means that we are being *conformed* to the image of God. It also means that we are being *protected* by God, *guided* by Him, that we have His *power* available to us, and a *love* within us that is not our own. These are essential qualities that are going to help us live the Christian life (Maxie Dunnam, *Alive in Christ*, The Upper Room, 1986).

The Will of God

We have thus far in this workbook set the stage for turning our wills and lives over to God, letting Him determine what is best for us. We have agreed to "let go" and quit trying to control the outcome of things. We have decided that God does a better job at being God than we do. But what then can we expect Him to do? What do we mean by God's will for our lives?

Gary Friesen, in his book *Decision Making and the Will of God*, says:

> God's individual will is that ideal, detailed life-plan which God has uniquely designed for each believer. This life-plan encompasses every decision we make and is the basis of God's daily guidance. This guidance is given through the indwelling Holy Spirit who progressively reveals God's life-plan to the heart of the individual believer. The Spirit uses many means to reveal this life-plan as we shall see, but He always gives confirmation at the point of each decision (Multnomah Press, 1980, p. 35).

One aspect of knowing God's will for our lives is very simple. It is found in direct statements of Scripture. For instance, it is God's will that:

- we choose to do His will (John 7:17),
- we be delivered out of the wicked world (Galatians 1:4),
- we be filled with the Holy Spirit (Ephesians 5:17),
- we avoid all sexual impurity (1 Thessalonians 4:3),
- we give thanks in all circumstances (1 Thessalonians 5:18).

But this still doesn't answer the question of how we will know God's will in other areas of our lives. It is reassuring to know that God cares about us, that He will guide us, and that He has an ideal plan for our lives, but it can be like charting a course through a maze to find that ideal plan.

Finding God's perfect plan for the individual has never been a simple task, so if you struggle with this concept, you are not alone. Most agree, however, that God's plan is best determined by using four primary principles:

1. *God's Word.* Nothing should short-circuit the important process of Bible study. Look for passages that deal with the subjects about which you are seeking God's will.

2. *Prayer.* Spend deliberate prayer time on a consistent basis, establishing a closer relationship with God. Ask God specifically for indications of His will.

3. *Circumstances.* Watch to see what doors open and which ones close. Not all open doors are God's will, but if something is God's will, He will open a door.

4. *Counsel.* Listen to the counsel of a wise friend (this might very well be your wife), pastor, or counselor. Remember, the value of counsel is only as good as the character of the one giving the counsel.

If we will practice these principles consistently, we will begin to sense God's presence and direction in our lives. As we sense His guidance, we should also practice accepting His guidance.

A helpful practice for accepting God's will is an exercise to bring ourselves to the point where we have no will of our own. When we do this, we can honestly say, "I am willing to do the will of God. Not my will, but Thy will be done." One way to do this is to take any proposal and write it down on the top of a piece of paper. Draw a vertical line down the center of the page. Then, in the left column, list all the reasons and benefits you can think of why you should take the proposed action. Then on the right side, opposite each positive reason, list a reason or benefit you would derive if you did not take the proposed action. Work at it until you have an equal number of reasons on both sides, and then you can say, "I have no will of my own. I can see an equal number of benefits either way."

Here is just one final concept concerning knowing the will of God: *The will of God will always be in harmony with the Spirit of God and the Word of God.* If we think that the Spirit of God has led us to do a certain thing, and yet the Word of God is opposed to what we are about to do, we can be certain it is not the will of God. We see the parallel and harmony of the Word of God and the Spirit of God when we compare two Scripture passages—Ephesians 5:18-20 and Colossians 3:16-17. A careful reading of each shows that being filled with the Holy Spirit and being filled with the Word of God are the same thing with the same results.

Self-Exploration

"Blessed is the man who does not walk in the counsel of the wicked. . . . But his delight is in the law of the Lord, and in His law he meditates day and night" (Psalm 1:1-2).

● What is your experience of meditation? _____

_____

_____

"Evening, and morning, and at noon, will I pray, and cry aloud, and He shall hear me" (Psalm 55:17).

● That is David's prayer schedule—what is yours? _____

_____

_____

● How has your prayer life changed as a result of your work in the Twelve Step program? _____

_____

_____

● Have you sensed God's guidance in your life at any particular time? Explain:

_____

_____

_____

_____

● Give an example of how God answered one of your prayers: _____

_____

_____

_____

"Your word is a lamp to my feet and a light to my path" (Psalm 119:105).

● What does that Scripture mean to you? _____

_____

_____

● What are some decisions you are wrestling with now, with which you would like God's help? _____

_____

_____

_____

● What are the steps you use to determine if something is the will of God?

_____

_____

_____

Step Eleven Application

We sought through prayer and meditation to improve our conscious contact with God as we understood Him, praying only for knowledge of His will for us and the power to carry it out.

"Let the word of Christ dwell in you richly" (Colossians 3:16a).

The entire Twelve Step program is built on our relationship with God, and so it should come as no surprise that in order to maintain the progress that we have made thus far, we must maintain our contact with God. To have contact with God demands that we set aside the thoughts, plans, and dreams that occupy our minds throughout the day. Instead, we need to focus on God.

For most of us, quieting ourselves and creating spaces of solitude are the biggest challenges we have. We have succeeded in busying ourselves and in convincing ourselves that we need to be that busy. "Who will watch the kids?" "There is work to do!" "I want to spend a little time relaxing by watching some television." The excuses are endless. We may be afraid to be alone with ourselves and God.

You will notice that the focus of a Christian's prayer life is not a laundry list of desires on our part, but rather knowledge of God's will and the power to carry it out. As our focus moves away from self, we become more concerned with God's desires in this troubled world. Of course, we benefit too. We receive the joy of fellowship with Him and His continual presence in our lives.

Most of us have taken considerable time off from relating to God. I (Dave) have given a lot of thought to how God must feel about this. On the one hand, I suspect He is grieved by our absence. However, the story of the Prodigal Son (Luke 15) suggests that He is delighted whenever we choose to return to Him. I don't think he ever expects us to be anything less than human. So, let's not beat ourselves up over our absences from Him, but rather keep returning to Him.

The Twelve Steps for Christians gives the following guidelines for prayer and meditating on God's Word:

At the beginning of the day, review your plans, and:
- Ask God for direction in your thoughts and actions
  - To keep you free from self-pity, dishonesty, and selfishness;
  - To provide the guidance needed to take care of any problems.
- Ask God for freedom from self-will
  - To prevent making requests unless others will be helped;
  - To avoid praying for our own selfish needs.

During the day, in moments of indecision or fear:
- Ask God for inspiration and guidance.
- Reflect on Step Three and turn it over.
  - Relax and breathe deeply several times.

—Be aware of any desire to struggle with a situation or person.
- Pray to God as often as necessary during the day.
  —"God please remove this_____" (feeling, obsession, addiction)
  —"Lord, not my will but Yours be done."
- If possible, call a support person to identify and share what is happening.

At the end of the day, review the events that happened, and:
- Reflect on Step Ten and take a personal inventory.
  —Ask God for guidance in taking corrective action.
- Ask God for knowledge of His will for you.
- Ask God's forgiveness where needed, and acknowledge that this review is not intended to cause obsessive thinking, worry, remorse, or morbid thinking.
- Give thanks to God for guidance and blessings that were part of the day (Recovery Publications, 1988, p. 112).

Professional Experience

It is with sadness that I (Dave) see so many people who are not yet ready to turn their wills and lives over to God. They still believe that they can find the answers necessary to make their lives work. "Things have worked out for me so far," they say. "Why should I change anything?"

Perhaps things will continue to work out for these people. But, in my experience, we all reach a time when our own resources just don't fill the bill. Then we reach out to the One who does have all the answers.

Prayer and meditation don't answer all of life's problems for us. What they do is to equip us to put things in perspective; to "let go" and quit struggling against that which we cannot control; to "turn it over." The truth is, we all need some extra help sometimes. The sooner we learn that truth, the better.

Recovery Affirmations

Step Eleven asks us to continue in daily seeking God, meditating, and reviewing our lives for changes that need to be made. If we will do these things, we will be taking active steps toward a rich spiritual life. We must be prepared for the "dry times," when we take control of our lives back from God, but He waits with open arms for us to return to Him.

This week, on a daily basis, affirm again that:

I am loved by God and am His child;

- Prayer and meditation keep me in contact with God;

  He has a plan for my life;

- He wants to protect, guide, empower, and love me;

- Should I fall away, He anticipates my return to Him.

Eleventh Step Prayer

Dear God,

Forgive me for continuing to try to do things on my own. When I start feeling stronger, I forget to rely on You. Thank You for waiting to take me back with open arms. Now, Lord, give me knowledge of Your will and the power to carry it out.

Amen.

Twelve

Men, Fitness, and Sexuality

As we have said before, those of you who take the time to read this book, complete its pages, and strive to live above your previous level are part of a select minority. You have grown in awareness, and the more work you do, the more aware you become. You have started a growth process which will not likely end.

I (Dave) am not one who is able to work with fabrics of any kind. I am intrigued, however, at what a good weaver is able to produce. A good weaver is able to take a variety of different materials and weave them together to form patterns. Close inspection reveals that the different materials remain distinct and yet formed in such a way as to come together to create a uniform product. The final result is often something quite beautiful.

I think our lives are like a tapestry, with many different parts, hopefully, coming together to form a uniform product. Unfortunately, what happens to many of us is that we ignore certain parts of our lives, become unbalanced, and this then creates crisis. Emotional and spiritual health require sensitivity to the various areas of our lives, and constant review to see if they are in balance.

Fitness

By now, you have hopefully begun to see that recovery involves the whole person, each strand of the tapestry. If any parts are not well, the whole thing is not well. Two areas easy to overlook until there is a crisis are fitness and sexuality. We want to look at the area of fitness now and hopefully avert a crisis before it occurs.

Exercise or physical labor has always been God's intention for man. It is interesting to us that God requires man to eat his food by the sweat of his brow (Genesis 3:19). Today only about 2 percent of the American population work on a farm. Many men have office jobs where they sit all day talking on the phone or typing data into a computer. So now, in order to reap the benefits of physical labor, we have to go to our local health club or spa to work up a sweat so we can maintain our cardiovascular health.

The benefits of physical fitness are well-documented, and exercise programs are advocated by doctors, nurses, dietitians, and mental health professionals. Health clubs and exercise gyms have sprung up all over the country offering aerobic exercise and weight room-type facilities—all with the goal of getting people in shape physically. Some people even become addicted to the benefits and physical stimulation that athletic exercise provides. However, as with any beneficial activity, we need to keep it in balance.

The Apostle Paul gives us the proper perspective of exercise when he uses an athletic metaphor in explaining how to train ourselves in godliness. He writes to Timothy, "Train yourself to be godly. For physical training is of some value, but godliness has value for all things, holding promise for both the present life and the life to come" (1 Timothy 4:7-8). Physical exercise is of value in this present life, but eternal benefits are our reward when we exercise ourselves in godliness. The same self-discipline we employ to maintain our exercise program should also be used to maintain our spiritual disciplines. Another way of saying it is, we should apply the same or greater effort that we use to maintain our cardiovascular health to working our recovery program.

It is exciting to read the Gospels and to see that Christ was very interested in the whole person. He wanted people whole, soul and body. He was so concerned about their well-being that He regularly healed the sick (Luke 9:2). And Paul reminds us that our bodies are "the temple of the Holy Spirit" (1 Corinthians 6:19). This alone would be reason enough to take good care of our bodies.

God, in His wisdom, seems to have made each part interdependent on the other parts. In other words, when I am physically feeling down, this will have an effect on my emotional and spiritual well-being. When I am emotionally down, the other aspects of my nature will be affected, and so on. The obvious point, then, is that we need to take care of each part of our nature. Physically, for your age and stature, there is a minimal requirement to be in the best condition possible. Are you doing everything you can to adequately maintain the "hardware" you were given? Is it time to consult a physician to see if you need to be engaging in more exercise?

Sexuality

Though this area was saved for the last chapter, it is not a subject of little importance. For a topic that is rarely, if ever, discussed openly in church circles, it causes more problems, perhaps, than any other issue.

Sexuality is not discussed openly very often because it is so personal, and we are uncomfortable discussing things at that level. Men sometimes think of it as an enemy. It is something to be feared, controlled, mistrusted, perhaps even avoided. How do we view the sexual side of our nature? Do we see our sexuality as a gift of God? Or do we see it as a curse from Satan? Or is it somewhere in between?

Where we learn about sex will affect our attitude toward it. Often our information comes from wrong sources and awkward situations. Where did you learn the nitty-gritty details about sex? High school health class? I (Ross) learned a great deal from the discussions at the play shed in Verdugo Park and from the drawings on the public restroom wall. Once, in response to a question of mine, my father gave me a book on human sexuality, but he rarely talked about it. The impression I received from my parents was that sex was something they had going between them, and that it was very special and too private to talk about.

Even though I had what I would call a fairly healthy view of sex, I wasn't prepared for Paul's explanation of a person's sex drive in 1 Corinthians 7. He says it is a gift of God. Yes, a gift of God—check it out in 1 Corinthians 7:7. It comes up in the context of deciding to marry or not to marry. Paul would like more people to serve God without the distractions that marriage causes but he is quick to state that if you have a strong sex drive, you should get married. "It is better to marry than to burn" is how he puts it. "But every man has his proper gift of God, one after this manner, and another after that" (v. 7, KJV). One manner is the gift of strong sexual passions, the other is the gift of little sexual desire.

If a Christian has little sexual desire, he should serve Christ as a single person. Otherwise, he should marry—it is the gift of God. If you looked up the term *gift* in the Greek, it is the word *charisma*. In all the seminars and sermons I have heard on charismatic gifts, I have never seen sexuality on the list of gifts. It is on God's list.

Sexuality, in some ways, is really something quite simple, and with us wherever male and female are together. Sexuality also has to do with maleness and femaleness. It has to do with the qualities that make men different from women.

Perhaps the central problem that faces all of us today concerns the question of values as it pertains to sexuality. In other words, is sexuality simply for personal pleasure, not to be taken too seriously, or are there to be values surrounding sexual expression? What are the rules of the game? Is sex and sexuality something which should exist only within the boundaries of relationship and marriage?

Steven Hayner, in an article entitled "What Dr. Ruth Couldn't Tell You," affirms a number of truths which are appropriate to the topic. They are as follows:

1. Our bodies and our sexuality were God's idea. The Creation account confirms that God made us male and female, and everything He made was very good.

2. God wants us to express our sexuality according to His intentions, without shame. There is no need to feel embarrassment or shame about our sexual desires.

3. Sexuality is an integral part of life. Every part of us is connected to every other part. We are physical, emotional, social, mental, sexual, spiritual beings.

4. God made sex to be part of a permanent, all-embracing relationship. Sex is not simply a biological or genital act (*Discipleship Journal,* Issue 64, 1991, p. 24).

While these are truths we all embrace, what can we do if we have violated some of these values? Perhaps we have "crossed the line" somewhere and want healing in our sexual lives. For many men the areas of the biggest struggles have to do with lust, masturbation, pornography, and the temptation to have an affair. Those who have succumbed to those temptations tell us that things are not at all what they are cracked up to be. The grass was not as green across the fence as it first appeared. The momentary satisfaction of indulging in fleshly lusts dissolves into an aftertaste of guilt and emptiness.

Allen shares his thoughts on his ordeal: "I had gotten to the point where my marriage simply felt stale to me. I knew I could work to liven things up, but why do that when someone else was available to make me feel better right now? I gave in and at first was glad I did. I didn't anticipate how quickly the excitement would fade and how hard it would be to put the pieces back together again. There is no going back.

"Now I am again working on my marriage, but I have to live with the truth that I devastated my wife and kids. I did something terribly selfish for my own pleasure. And in the long run, it didn't solve a thing."

If you are tempted to have an affair, or have had one and want to get on with your life, the task is now to put energy into building a healthy marital relationship. There are no shortcuts to a happy, healthy marriage. We must be prepared to count the cost of "crossing the lines," remembering that the price simply is not worth it. We also need to stay close to God. It is as we drift away from His guidance and protection that we get into trouble.

Sexual Addiction

Though it is never enjoyable to admit to any addiction, in the admission is the first step toward freedom. Several years ago Patrick Carnes, in his book *Out of the Shadows* (CompCare, 1983), introduced the topic of sexual addictions. In it he detailed the stages men go through who are struggling with sexual addictions. He indicated that there are many men who are involved in compulsive sexual behaviors which are destructive to them and their families.

These men's lives are controlled by sex in much the same way that a drug addict is controlled by drugs. Their lives are centered around when they will achieve their next sexual encounter. Their fantasies are fed by pornography, television, compulsive masturbation. While it may be tempting to think that it only happens to men "from the other side of the tracks," think again.

What is the solution? Again, there is help available, and there are steps that can be taken to recover from sexual addiction. Recovery involves:

1. Naming the addiction;
2. Seeking support from Sexual Addicts Anonymous or some professional resource;
3. Repentance, and seeking godly counsel and support;
4. Learning places of vulnerability and changing your lifestyle accordingly.

This problem is rampant in our society today, but if men will stand up and acknowledge that they struggle in this area, we believe there will be increased freedom from sexual sins and compulsions. There is a prayer that may be very helpful to those who struggle in this area. It bears repeating on a daily basis.

> Heavenly Father, You understand the scars on my soul from misused sex. "O Lord, hear my prayer, listen to my cry for mercy; in Your faithfulness and righteousness come to my relief. Do not bring Your servant into judgment, for no one living is righteous before You" (Psalm 143:1-2). Bring hope and help and healing into my life.
>
> I affirm that it is Your will that I should be holy in regard to sex, honesty, and truth. Help me to drop my defenses before You and humbly follow Your direction in finding expert Christian counsel. Teach me (and help me learn) to control my body in a way that is holy and honorable and not in passionate lust like the heathen who do not know God.
>
> Where I have been victimized, I appeal to you as my strength. "Rescue me from my enemies, O Lord, for I hide myself in You" (Psalm 143:9). Where I have victimized others, I honestly repent and turn from my sin. I trust You in simple and wholehearted faith, Lord Jesus. "Teach me to do Your will, for You are my God; may Your good Spirit lead me on level ground" (Psalm 143:10). In the mighty name of the Lord Jesus Christ I pray. Amen (*Running the Red Lights,* Charles Mylander, Regal Books, 1986, pp. 189-190).

Most men have failed in the area of sexuality in one way or another. The important thing to remember is that God offers us grace and tells us to try again. Encourage yourself with the words of Jesus to the woman caught in adultery. "Jesus straightened up and asked her, 'Woman, where are they? Has no one condemned you?' 'No one, sir,' she said. 'Then neither do I condemn you. . . . Go now and leave your life of sin' " (John 8:10-11). It is as we take off our masks of self-deception and experience God's forgiving grace that we can truly begin again.

Self-Exploration

● What are your physical fitness goals? _____

_____

_____

● What is your ideal weight and how close are you to it? _____

_____

_____

● What impressions did you get from your parents concerning sex? _____

_____

_____

_____

● Where did you learn about sex, and where would you go now if you had a question?

_____

_____

_____

● Solomon speaks with candor and openness about sexual expressions in marriage. What is his main thought in Proverbs 5:15-21? _____

_____

_____

● What has been your experience with "crossing the lines" sexually? _____

_____

_____

_____

● What are your fears about sharing that story with someone?_____

_____

_____

Step Twelve Application

Having had a spiritual awakening as a result of these steps, we tried to carry this message to others and to practice these principles in all our affairs.

"Brothers, if someone is caught in a sin, you who are spiritual should restore him gently. But watch yourself, or you also may be tempted" (Galatians 6:1).

At this point in the Twelve Step program, you have done a lot of work. You have seen that there will be triumphs, and there will be setbacks. All in all, we really do work the program "one day at a time." But through it all, we've learned that reliance on God is the only way to go. We cannot control the way life comes to us, and we have had to learn to take what comes as a gift from God. Sometimes the lessons are sweet, sometimes painful, but always for the purpose of helping us to grow.

Step Twelve tells us that we will carry the message on to others. But what is the message? It is a message of being affirmed, understood, and accepted by God. And it is a message that we can rise above our addictions and dysfunctional traits and learn new ways of caring for ourselves and others. We want to pass on the message that the values held up by the world are not the values that work, and that there are better ways to live.

We must not take lightly the fact that we have hope to share with others at a time when someone may desperately need to hear an encouraging word. We are able now to offer them some of the principles that we have used to help us in our times of trouble. We can share how each one of the steps enhanced our walk with the Lord. Beginning back with the First Step, we learned about how powerless we really are. Steps Two and

Three directed us to the source of power, God. Steps Four through Nine helped us to take an inventory of our lives, looking for patterns that created trouble for us. Steps Ten and Eleven were the "maintenance" steps to keep our walk with God stable. Finally, Step Twelve encourages us to pass on this hope to others, as we ourselves continue to practice the principles in all our relationships.

Our difficulties, these Steps, and other people we've shared ourselves with have been instrumental in our making decisions to change our lives. God wanted to get our attention in order to show us that there is a more rewarding way to live. We must remember where we have been so that we are not tempted to drift back into old ways of living. If we do drift, we have past experiences to remind us of the choices we can make to improve our circumstances.

"At one time we too were foolish, disobedient, deceived, and enslaved by all kinds of passions and pleasures. But when the kindness and love of God our Savior appeared, He saved us, not because of righteous things we had done, but because of His mercy. He saved us through the washing of rebirth and renewal by the Holy Spirit, whom He poured out on us generously through Jesus Christ our Savior, so that having been justified by His grace, we might become heirs having the hope of eternal life" (Titus 3:3-7).

The renewal of the Holy Spirit is a lifelong process. Our program with the Twelve Steps is an expression of that continual renewal.

Character defects and addictive tendencies show up at different levels. It is like peeling an onion. As we go through the Twelve Steps, we peel back a layer and deal with it. The amazing thing is, that as we again go over the Twelve Steps, another layer is peeled back. We gain deeper insights and increase our understanding. It is an ever-increasing and growing process.

Professional Experience

Each new day can be seen as a gift from God. It is not just a day to control and to make things turn out the way we want them to be. That kind of approach is bound to create frustration. On the other hand, we do not have to sit back passively either and just let things happen to us. As is often the case, balance is the key.

We now have a heightened level of awareness. We can now make more informed choices about our lives. We will have a better sense as to when we should push for something to happen, and when we should let go and let things develop naturally.

Remember that we are complicated creatures. There are many aspects to our personages. Each area of our lives affects the other areas. If we will give attention to each area, the other aspects of our lives will benefit as well.

Recovery Affirmations

It is important to repeatedly remind ourselves just how much we have accomplished. When we feel discouraged and haven't completed what we might have hoped, we need to remind ourselves what we have accomplished with God's help. We need to focus on what God has done for us.

We cannot wait for others to affirm us. Sometimes friends will be there for us, giving us an encouraging hand. Often, because they are caring for themselves, we will need to encourage ourselves. This is a skill that takes practice. We need to remind ourselves that we are special to God. He cares for us and is enabling us to grow. We need to follow David's example in Psalm 42 where he explains what he does when he is discouraged: "Why are you downcast, O my soul? Why so disturbed within me? Put your hope in God, for I will yet praise Him, my Savior and my God" (v. 5).

Each day this week affirm that:

- I am growing, and God is helping me become who He wants me to be;

- Struggles are here to help me to grow;

- I am a new creation;

- I can live in peace and serenity.

Prayer for Serenity

God, grant me the serenity
to accept the things I cannot change,
the courage to change the things I can,
and the wisdom to know the difference.
Living one day at a time,
enjoying one moment at a time;
accepting hardship as a pathway to peace;
taking, as Jesus did,
this sinful world as it is,
not as I would have it;
trusting that You will make all things right
if I surrender to Your will;
so that I may be reasonably happy in this life
and supremely happy with You forever in the next.

Amen.

Reinhold Niebuhr

Glossary of Terms

These are "working definitions," not dictionary definitions. This glossary describes how these terms "work out" in practice.

ABANDONMENT—When I feel someone has surrendered his caretaking responsibility to me. It is the result of feeling that a commitment has been broken to "be there," to meet my deep, personal needs.

ABUSE—Any experience in a relationship which does not contribute to one's growth or well-being. Abuse may range in intensity from a "less-than-nurturing" relationship to a violent, destructive relationship. It is most damaging when it occurs in childhood.

ADDICTION—Any obsession, compulsion, or preoccupation which enslaves a person's desire or will. It is the habitual resort to the same means of relieving personal pain.

APPROPRIATE—Meeting a legitimate need in a legitimate way. *Inappropriate* is meeting a legitimate need in an illegitimate way.

BOUNDARIES—The limits that define my personal territory. They clarify who I am and what I value. There are external (i.e., physical, sexual) boundaries and there are internal (i.e., thinking, feeling, choosing) boundaries. These define my "space" and "comfort zones," allowing me to let people in or keep them out as I choose. They also define my respect of others' "space" and "comfort zones." They are the limits I set regarding things that are important to me.

CARETAKING—Being responsible for the care and well-being of another. This concern seeks to meet both physical and emotional needs.

CODEPENDENT—Taking inordinate responsibility for another by compulsively rescuing them, while neglecting one's own best interest. Codependency is inappropriate caretaking which enables another to continue in destructive behavior.

COMPULSIVE—Impulsive acts beyond one's conscious control. It is behaviors or thoughts which occur automatically, without conscious choice. It is the opposite of freedom. The severity of the habit often intensifies over time.

CONTROL—Any attempt to manage people or events to guarantee a desired outcome. It is seeking to regulate things or people to be the way I think they ought to be.

CONVERSION—A change in perspective, attitude, and behavior as the result of a change of belief. It is usually precipitated when something I value is threatened or lost if I do not change.

DENIAL—The refusal to acknowledge some truth about myself or my situation. It differs from a *blind spot* in that it is something I see but refuse to fully acknowledge.

DEPENDENCY NEEDS—Needs that I have that I cannot meet myself, but must be provided by another person. They include emotional nurturing (comfort, encouragement, and approval) as well as physical nurturing (medical/dental attention, sex, and financial resources).

DYSFUNCTIONAL—Any relationship that is impaired because I do not have the freedom to think, feel, trust, and talk about what is happening with me. In a dysfunctional relationship there is no freedom to truly be myself. Reality is changed to appear to be what the dysfunctional person wants it to be.

ENMESHMENT—Becoming overly involved and entangled in another's life, to the point where confusion develops as to who is meeting whose needs, and individuality is lost. One example is the parent who becomes enmeshed with the child by taking total care of him, never allowing the child to develop the ability to make his own choices. The child meets the parent's needs when it is the parent who should be meeting the child's needs.

EMPOWERMENT—The growing belief that with God's help I can accomplish that which is important to me.

FANTASY—An imagined reality to compensate for or replace one's own painful reality. It is usually initiated by parents attacking, denying, or ignoring a child's expression of his reality, teaching him that it is not appropriate or safe to express it.

FORGIVENESS—Letting go of the desire for revenge or compensation for an offense. It is the basis for restoring a broken relationship.

GUILT—The awareness and condition of knowing that I have violated some standard or boundary. Feeling remorse is the healthy response to having committed a breach of conduct. Guilt is the legitimate expression of the conscience. False guilt is the product of a miseducated conscience.

INTERDEPENDENCE—Recognizing the reciprocal nature of meeting needs. It is identifying my own needs and being willing to ask someone appropriate to meet them, while being available, when appropriate, to meet the needs of others.

INTIMACY—Sharing deep, personal aspects of my being with another person. It takes time and repeated risk to develop intimacy.

LETTING GO—The freedom and respect I give to others to manage their own lives. Understanding that the only person I can change is myself. I quit trying so hard to fix things.

MANIPULATION—Using emotional means (usually guilt) to get someone to do what I want. It is something the person would not do without emotional pressure. This kind of emotional pressure is often called emotional blackmail.

MEDITATION—Quiet listening to God. It is a private devotion consisting of deep, continual reflection on God and/or His Word.

MINIMIZATION—Downplaying or "sugar coating" a distasteful aspect of myself or my circumstances.

NEEDS—Those things I must have in order to grow into a mature, responsible adult. Needs are life-sustaining while wants are life-enhancing.

OFFENDER—One who violates the boundaries of another.

POWERLESSNESS—A helpless feeling I have when I realize those times that I don't have the ability to effect change in others or in my circumstances. I learn that I can influence my own feelings, thoughts, and values, but cannot control those same things in others. One of the major areas of powerlessness is my inability to control the consequences of my wrong decisions.

REALITY—The awareness of the true state of affairs. It is an accurate perception of the truth about myself and my circumstances. Dysfunctional reality has two levels. One involves hiding any reality from others for fear of it being unacceptable. The second involves not knowing my reality, so I make up one that I think will be acceptable.

RECOVERY—Gaining the skills to live successfully by learning to recognize and deal with my dysfunctional traits. I am growing in my ability to identify my needs and wants, and to define the values that are important to me. I am in recovery when I am able to let go of my feelings about the hurtful events of my past. Ultimately, recovery is growing strong in my relationship with the Lord.

RELIGIOSITY—Having all the external trappings of religion, with little of the internal experience of a relationship with God.

RITUALIZATION—Familiar patterns of behavior used repeatedly to achieve a desired result. Rituals can range from positive family traditions to destructive patterns of dysfunctional behavior.

SELF-ESTEEM—The view one has of himself. Healthy self-esteem is the internal experiencing of one's own value as a person.

SELF-PARENTING—Taking responsibility for choices that are self-nurturing. Doing for myself what a responsible parent would do for me.

SERENITY—The peaceful feeling which comes when I accept where I am today. Living with my limits and losses without resentment.

SEXUALITY—Maleness and femaleness. Those qualities that make a man and woman unique and distinct from one another, socially, physically, emotionally, and spiritually.

SHAME—Fear of exposure of my humiliation, cowardice, or failure. There are two forms of shame: unhealthy or toxic shame, and healthy shame. Healthy shame tells me that I have limitations and causes me to deepen my trust in God. Toxic shame leaves me feeling exposed and "bad." This shame originally comes from childhood, when I expressed a need or want and I was made to feel shame for asking.

SUCCESS—Living with integrity.

VICTIMIZATION—Occurs when a major personal boundary is forcefully transgressed. The violation of personal boundaries may be emotional, physical, or sexual, and results in trauma. Abuse is the term for the acts of the perpetrator, while victimization is the term for the recipient of the abuse.

VULNERABILITY—Being open about my reality. This repeatedly puts me at risk for rejection. I do this in hopes of gaining intimacy.

Forming A Men's Christian Twelve Step Group

A decision to form a Men's Christian Twelve Step group in your church, or perhaps in your community, is a very exciting move, sure to yield valuable results. It is possible to combine the healing principles found in Scripture with the structure of the Twelve Step movement. In this group, however, the "higher power" is Jesus Christ. We are seeking to obey Paul's instruction to Timothy to flee destructive lusts and to follow righteousness, faith, love, and peace with other men who are seeking God with a pure heart (2 Timothy 2:22).

If there is anything that the national men's movement has taught us, it is how desperately alone most men feel, and the genuine need they have to meet with other men to gain a sense of understanding and belonging. Unfortunately, very few resources exit where men can meet to work on themselves, utilizing Christian principles. There is a desperate need for more groups such as this both inside and outside the organized church, where men can bear one another's burdens and so fulfill the law of Christ (Galatians 6:2).

However, forming a men's group is often not as easy as it first sounds. While men are longing to belong to such a group, they are also generally quite guarded and have cultural defenses in place which tell them not to share their personal feelings with anyone. It is common, then, for men to have to be invited into such a group by someone who they already know and trust. A blanket invitation is not likely to draw many to the group. If the group is to be part of the ongoing life of a particular church, it will also be important for the church to give the group an outright endorsement. The group must not be hidden away as if it is some "step child" of the body.

The traditional Twelve Step program recommends some structure which has been found helpful, so that all members are likely to have many of their needs met. A lack of structure may have positive benefits in the short run, but some time later the group will likely begin to dissolve for lack of leadership and direction. It is best that there be a facilitator who sets the direction for the group. Many have found it helpful to rotate the leadership of the group from week to week. It is important for the life of the group that there be an express purpose to the group, clear leadership, and direction. Within those guidelines, the group can be free to take on its own particular life. No one group is exactly like another.

After deciding to form a group, a decision must be made as to its focus. This workbook is presented in such a manner as to present topics that can be discussed and personalized at the group's pace. There are other topics that can be equally effective to draw men together for a sense of commitment to one another. The Twelve Step program has an agenda similar to, but different from, the one we are describing here.

Simply studying the Twelve Steps and applying them to current life circumstances has always been found beneficial. Again, the important factors are the opportunity for men to gather, be truly heard, and learn to listen and support one another. Those willing to make the commitment to meet for an indefinite period of time, on a consistent basis, will reap rich rewards.

A group will tend to be more cohesive and functional if a few guidelines are met. They include:

- That group members have a shared purpose, perhaps simply to work through this workbook together;
- That there be a commitment to be vulnerable with one another, sharing feelings and attempting to be honest in all they say and do;
- That all agree they need to change, and are there to humbly work on themselves in some way;
- That all agree to be accountable to one another, sharing insights and perceptions at appropriate times;
- That all agree to hold confidential what is said in the group;
- That all agree to make a commitment of time to meet consistently with other group members;
- That all agree to suspend negative judgment about the group process, others' problems, and topics as they are introduced.

A Twelve Step group is usually a place where "counseling" and advice is kept to a minimum, and acceptance and caring are maximized. Confidence is placed in the Holy Spirit to direct each member's participation. Strength is given by the group to each participant by their active listening, obvious care and concern, and the prayer each gives for the others. Members show their care by focusing on the person speaking, asking leading questions, and accepting the other's point of view even if it differs from their own. This is fulfilling Paul's exhortation to encourage the fainthearted, to support the weak, and to be patient toward all men (1 Thessalonians 5:14). In this environment members feel free to share innermost feelings and thoughts, and are loved and ultimately healed.

Perhaps the most powerful way to show care and concern for group members is to contact them between meetings, simply to ask them how they are doing. This "connection" truly binds members to each other and is tremendously healing. Members are encouraged to reach out to one another between meetings if they have a special need.

Time must be taken between meetings to complete the written assignments. In that way participants are ready to share their answers at the time of the meeting. This is probably the most effective use of the time together. Many groups have found it inspiring to close the group with either the Serenity Prayer or the Lord's Prayer. The uniqueness of these groups certainly comes from the strength we have in meeting as Christians. Do not forget to call on the Lord to help determine the needs of each particular meeting.

Recommended Reading

Alcorn, Randy. *Money, Possessions and Eternity.* Tyndale House Publishers, Inc., Wheaton, Illinois, 1989.

Augsburger, David. *Caring Enough to Confront.* Regal Books, Ventura, California, 1980.

Augsburger, David. *Caring Enough to Forgive.* Regal Books, Ventura, California, 1981.

Baker, Don. *Acceptance.* Multnomah Press, Portland, Oregon, 1977.

Beattie, Melody. *Codependent No More.* Hazelden Foundation, New York, New York, 1987.

Beattie, Melody. *The Language of Letting Go.* Hazelden Foundation, New York, New York, 1990.

Beattie, Melody. *Codependents' Guide to the Twelve Steps.* Prentice-Hall/Parkside Recovery Books, New York, New York, 1990.

Bradshaw, John. *Bradshaw On: The Family.* Health Communications, Inc., Deerfield Beach, Florida, 1988.

Bradshaw, John. *Healing the Shame That Binds.* Health Communications, Inc., Deerfield Beach, Florida, 1988.

Campolo, Tony. *The Power Delusion.* Victor Books, Wheaton, Illinois, 1983.

Carnes, Patrick, *Out of the Shadows.* CompCare Publishers, Minneapolis, Minnesota, 1983.

Covey, Stephen. *The 7 Habits of Highly Effective People.* Simon and Schuster, New York, New York, 1990.

Crabb, Larry. *Inside Out.* NavPress, Colorado Springs, Colorado, 1988.

Dalbey, Gordon. *Healing the Masculine Soul.* Word Publishing, Dallas, Texas, 1988.

Eisenman, Tom. *Temptations Men Face.* InterVarsity Press, Downers Grove, Illinois, 1990.

Ellul, Jacques. *Money and Power.* InterVarsity Press, Downers Grove, Illinois, 1984.

Friends In Recovery. *The Twelve Steps for Christians.* Recovery Publications, San Diego, California, 1988.

Hershey, Terry. *Go Away, Come Closer.* Word Publishing, Dallas, Texas, 1990.

Hybels, Bill. *Honest to God.* Zondervan Books, Grand Rapids, Michigan, 1990.

Joy, Donald. *Men Under Construction.* Victor Books, Wheaton, Illinois, available spring 1993.

Keen, Sam. *Fire in the Belly.* Bantam Books, New York, New York, 1991.

Kritsberg, Wayne. *Healing Together.* Health Communications, Inc., Deerfield Beach, Florida, 1990.

May, Gerald. *Addiction and Grace.* Harper Collins Publishers, San Francisco, California, 1988.

McGee, Robert S. *The Search for Significance.* Rapha Publishing, Houston, Texas, 1990.

Miller, Keith. *A Hunger for Healing.* Harper Collins, San Francisco, California, 1991.

Mylander, Charles. *Running the Red Lights.* Regal Books, Ventura, California, 1986.

Peck, M. Scott. *The Road Less Travelled.* Simon and Schuster, New York, New York, 1978.

Perkins, Bill. *Fatal Attraction.* Harvest House Publishers, Eugene, Oregon, 1991.

Robinson, Bryan E. *Work Addiction.* Health Communications, Inc., Deerfield Beach, Florida, 1989.

Seamands, David, *Healing for Damaged Emotions.* Victor Books, Wheaton, Illinois, 1981.

Smalley, Gary and John Trent. *The Blessing.* Thomas Nelson, Nashville, Tennessee, 1986.

Wegscheider-Cruse, Sharon. *Learning to Love Yourself.* Health Communications, Inc., Deerfield Beach, Florida, 1987.

Wegscheider-Cruse, Sharon. *Another Chance.* Health Communications, Inc., Deerfield Beach, Florida, 1987.

Wegscheider-Cruse, Sharon. *Coupleship.* Health Communications, Inc., Deerfield Beach, Florida, 1987.

Woititz, Janet G. *Struggle for Intimacy.* Health Communications, Inc., Pompano Beach, Florida, 1985.

RECLAIMING MANHOOD SEMINARS

Dr. David Hawkins and Ross Tunnell
are available to your church or men's group for:

- *Seminars*
- *Retreats*
- *Conferences*

- *Conventions*
- *Workshops*
- *Consultation*

You can reach *Reclaiming Manhood Seminars*
by writing to either:

Portland Counseling Services
P.O. Box 66374
Portland, OR 97226-0374

or

Northwest Counseling Services
1414 16th Avenue
Longview, WA 98632